CW01310355

Dear Gillian

With kind regards
and best wishes

ANDREW NEIL SPRIGGS

The Two Shadows of Success

Andrew Spriggs

authorHOUSE®

AuthorHouse™ UK
1663 Liberty Drive
Bloomington, IN 47403 USA
www.authorhouse.co.uk
Phone: 0800.197.4150

© 2016 Andrew Spriggs. All rights reserved.

No part of this book may be reproduced, stored in a retrieval system, or transmitted by any means without the written permission of the author.

Published by AuthorHouse 07/05/2016

ISBN: 978-1-5246-3617-3 (sc)
ISBN: 978-1-5246-3619-7 (hc)
ISBN: 978-1-5246-3618-0 (e)

Library of Congress Control Number: 2016909993

Print information available on the last page.

Any people depicted in stock imagery provided by Thinkstock are models, and such images are being used for illustrative purposes only.
Certain stock imagery © Thinkstock.

This book is printed on acid-free paper.

Because of the dynamic nature of the Internet, any web addresses or links contained in this book may have changed since publication and may no longer be valid. The views expressed in this work are solely those of the author and do not necessarily reflect the views of the publisher, and the publisher hereby disclaims any responsibility for them.

Chapter 1

SCHOOL

Secondary school was for me a difficult time. I found fitting in and making friends difficult and had numerous problems that seemed to rear their ugly head every year of school – when one issue was resolved, another would appear. I lacked confidence in myself and I was in fact quite defence less – a lamb to the slaughterhouse. I was bullied from time to time and I found school uncomfortable at the best of times. Being told off felt like I'd committed the ultimate sin and that negation carried on to affect my self esteem. Being given a detention at lunch time on several occasions knocked a very fragile composure and I constantly sought approval and acceptance from others. I was fearful of my peers, teachers and even friends. I would never dare to stick up for myself and would cower when laughed at. My friends were at times quite against me and would ignore me and I just felt so powerless. I often went home crying and on one occasion my mum went into school to talk to my form tutor about how it was affecting me. Even my mum would say to stick up for myself and to not be so quick to allow friends back into my life when they so chose to. But I was who I was then and I had the fortune that, in spite of all the negative things that I had to withstand, I made some good longstanding friends, these being David Roberts and Steve Dodds. David was in my form throughout the first few years and then in year 11 the three of us became better friends after a school arranged night out. David is a very down to earth and generous guy who has stood by me following my diagnosis. Being totally none-judgemental and very supportive as well as caring, he has time after time proven himself to be a true a friend, along side his sisters Sammy and Leanne and their partners. He got married last year in 2015 and is married to the kindest and friendliest young lady, Silvi who is from Slovakia. They are now have a baby girl Grace and are indeed very happy. Steve is too is an amazing guy, the most resourceful guy I have ever come across- his quick witted razor sharp sense of humour do him proud. Steve has a lot to be proud of, he gained is doctorate in 2015 after leaving school at 16 and so had a considerably harder challenge to continue with higher education. Steve is well suited to his girlfriend Josie who also completed her PhD in 2015. He is too very supportive and between him and David they have been amazing. The transition into sixth form was easier and I enjoyed these two years more than the previous five as my good friendships became more established. I started to come out of my shell a bit, although I'd suffered a bit a long the way, I prepared to take my A levels. I dedicated a lot of time to researching universities and visited a few – Leeds, Nottingham, East Anglia, Queen Mary and Westfield College and Royal Holloway, (colleges of the University of London) amongst others. I remember when I got my results – a B in Geography, B in General Studies and C in French and C in Economics how disappointed I was. I needed a B in French to get me into my first choice, who rejected me which really angered me to the point where I slammed the phone down on the admissions tutor saying *"well thanks for nothing."* My second choice but when I rang them as my second choice they were non-committal, although they did say they would get back to me. However in the end I spoke to the Exams officer at school and had all papers re marked. The year before

I started university in upper sixth, I'd wanted to have a gap year and I'd missed the boat with various gap year deadlines. My last hope of a successful gap year placement was the hotel application I'd made to work in France, all the other deadlines had now passed. I remember a conversation that I had with my sister when she said that I'd better buck my ideas up towards the end of my A levels as I'd missed the majority of the gap year deadlines for applying to work or teach abroad. Towards the end of my A levels I received a letter back from the hotel chains I had written to say that they had passed my application onto the related Parisian hotels. Amazing I thought! Imagine living in Paris! I was getting really excited about the prospect of working abroad and soon was telling all my friends about it. And so soon after receiving a letters stating that my application had been forwarded onto an address for the Parisian hotels concerned, I received a letter offering an interview at one such Parisian hotel. My only other option at this point was to work for a company near Leicester in Ipstock, my last ditch attempt at succeeding with the year in industry programme. I'd only just recently had the interview there and had been advised by the interviewee to go to Paris for the interview. I spent the night before my trip in the middle of August at my parent's caravan in the Peak District; my dad drove my very early to Manchester airport to get the Air France flight to Paris. I dropped my things off at a hotel I'd booked (I'd booked this at a local travel agent in Chesterfield) in Courbevoie and went straight to the hotel. I was quite flabbergasted but I knew I had to accept the offer – I went for the interview as a waiter – I'd booked a weekend in Paris and Dad had taken me up to Manchester so that I could fly over direct to Charles de Gaulle. The interview was on this Friday with one of the Personnel Directors Monsieur Lefage. I attempted to answer his questions and tried to sound upbeat and positive although I had no idea what he was saying to me, except not to forget my locker key (which he said in English funnily enough) After the informal chat Mr Lefage walked me across to the restaurant where I had a mini tour and met the manager there, Monsieur Klosters. A typically French man with circular lenses in a three piece suit, he certainly looked the part. When I saw how big the restaurant was I realised how out of my depth I was! A previous pot washer who had done a trial shift in a local informal pub, I was beginning to feel quite anxious. However, in spite of my appalling French I got the job- I was over the moon, but I should think so given the distance I had travelled to get there! I now had two days to look for a flat – where the hell should I start looking in such a huge metropolis?! I decided that it might be best to look in Courbevoie where I was staying in a hotel. Where else should I look? I might as well have put a pin in a map and guessed! The area around Montparnasse is very lucrative and posh-this being the left bank. However rents in Paris are very high which did in fact narrow down my choice of where to start looking. The further out I would look however I would have to factor in travel expenses, although as Mr Lefage pointed out I would receive 50% back each month. On the Saturday I enquired at Condoive agency who showed me round a few flats and I accepted one which was opposite a leisure centre. It was a 15 minute walk to the station and wasn't ready to be inhabited- the landlady herself was doing work on the flat but for fear of not finding anything else I took it – this was a real adventure for me and I was very excited. On the Sunday I flew back home and told friends and family of my success.

Chapter 2

WORKING IN FRANCE

Two weeks later mum and dad took me to Birmingham International Airport and I said my goodbyes which we all found difficult. When I arrived at Paris Charles De Gaulle airport I struggled across to the RER where I went straight to the hotel fully laden with 5 bags, the porters were helpful and helped store them whilst I went to Condoive Immobilier to arrange the signing of the contract. That was to be the first night in my flat! It was quite a distance to be honest. I was lucky in the sense that Mathilda, a girl who worked in the estate agency spoke English as the Managing Director did not. Mathilda came with me, with my baggage to the flat where the landlady was finishing off the refurbishment. Fortunately the landlady left a sofa bed but the microwave did not work and there was no hot water for a shower. Mum had given me some recipes such as scrambled egg for breakfast which came to be a lifeline! The next day was an induction day, from 9 to 5pm with three others and Monsieur Duveau, the Personnel Director. Most of the day which started with being offered breakfast – croissants juice and coffee. I spent most of the time trying to understand what he was talking about. The other three – Elodie, Sandrine and another chap whose name I couldn't remember were all yapping away and after the induction I went to see Monsieur Klosters who confirmed my starting time for the next day as being 6.30am. When he said this I had no idea how I'd cope getting up that early! I later on worked out I'd need to get the 5.30am train from Courbevoie station into Paris St Lazare for 5.45am, then metro line 13 to Gaîté station (direction Chatillon Montrouge), to arrive at work at around 6am. The next day I woke up at 4.30am and bleary eyed and nervous I stepped into the cold shower – I had no hot water still and so this was quite painful particularly at this! I left the flat at 5.15am and got to the train station on time for the shuttle service to Paris St Lazare. It was pitch black – this was September 1st and everything was eerily spooky. The train arrived and 15 minutes later we arrived into Paris St Lazare, I found my way to the metro and then whoosh what a culture shock – it was full of foreign nationals going to work, largely French Africans – the first thing that became apparent was the smell – it did put me off to be honest, particularly at this time but what choice was there?! On arrival at the hotel I went down to the changing rooms and met my colleague to be, Paulo in the lift. This was where my French work experience began. I was met immediately on exiting the lift by Celine, who came across as a very forceful hard faced lady – but Celine was to become a real ally there. I was working with Pierre and Annabelle on the buffet. Pierre was quite a character and I sensed soon after starting that there was some tension between him and Celine. Annabelle was lovely, and explained what I had to do – basically refill all aspects of the buffet at this point. Little was I to know that there was far more to it than that! The restaurant could seat 250 people at any one time, and there was a continental, cold and hot buffet- croissants, chocolate croissants, pain aux raisin, toast, cold meat and cheese, yoghurts, and cooked American breakfast including bacon, sausages, all types of eggs, baked beans, tomatoes, mushrooms, omelettes and much more. The restaurant was after all 4 star. The rest of the team were placed at stations

– 2,3,4,5,6,7,8,9, these were manned by Robert, Colette, Nadège, Vincent, Rosanne, Serge, Simon, Aude and Andrea. There were then the head waitresses Juliette, Maude, Louis, Thomas, Celine, Pauline and Oscar.I also met and became good friends with Stephanie and Julia, two German girls who were waitresses and who I went onto live with. I came home from work that day, exhausted and went straight to bed. I don't even remember if I set my alarm, but the next morning I awoke and had the shock of my life, it was 6am when I woke! I had to be at the hotel for 6.30! How was I going to make it?! When I arrived 45 minutes late for work- I must have slept through my feeble alarm and raced – well as fast as the train and metro would take me to work and feeling panic stricken and fearful of the consequences of having overlaid especially on my second day!! I did get a ticking off from Maude, one of the Maître d'Hotels (Head waitresses) but said how sorry I was so it was soon forgotten. In the first of the monthly "reunions" I remember Louis saying that there were too many late arrivals by staff. Just before this reunion I got to know Stephanie and Julia. I got to know Stephanie first (although Id talked to Julia about her offering to join me on a French course) and on my first few says off, which were the same as hers – she was I believe my guardian angel out there – she always had my back – as did Julia too. On the Wednesday afternoon at 3pm when we finished for the week we agreed before finishing that we would meet up as her brother Andreas was coming to Paris. It was a real relief that Stephanie had the same days off as me. On the Thursday eve I met Stephanie and Andreas close to Chatelet-Les-Halles and we went to a restaurant / bar and had drinks. Stephanie and Andreas smoked, I still had managed to refrain however I have to admit it was tempting to start again. We had an enjoyable evening on Thursday evening, it was really nice to have met such people, as Paris can in fact be a really lonely place. Andreas was on holiday from being in the army – in Germany at this time it was mandatory although from what he was saying he was pretty fed up. It's with things like this that make me realise how lucky I am. We had a fun time and in particular listening to Stephanie say to beggars asking for cigarettes sarcastically that *"il y a un tabac là-bas"*, in so many words there is tobacco shop near by and that she had no intention of giving one out! The next day I went over to Stephanie's flat –it was quite a long journey from Courbevoie where by I had to change from the train at St.Lazare station to the metro and onto line 3 to Opéra then line 7 direction La Corneuve, metro station Corentin Cariou.It took about 1 hour in total. Stephanie and Julia lived in the 19th Arondissement which was notorious for crime and poverty, not surprisingly it was relatively cheap to live in. Stephanie paid just 2200 Francs per month – about £220 per month at this time and this included heating. The flat was more than double the size of mine, 80 square metres. My flat in Courbevoie was about an hour away on public transport from the hotel and I was paying 2800 Francs. Courbevoie, was in its banlieue situation quite significantly more affluent than 19th Arrondissement. But I didn't know anyone there and I was quite lonely. I found the journey to work tiring and cumbersome, although when all said and done it was a quicker journey than from the 19th Arrondissement to work. It was actually quite trendy but I guess I had my reservations. Stephanie and Julia came over to my flat a few weeks later for dinner and I remember Julia discussing that the flat I had would suit her partner Herbert. I got to know Herbert a few months later in October when Stephanie and Julia made me an offer I could not refuse – they had a spare room and asked if I'd like to move in with them! Of course I wanted to but I was tied to the contract I had with my flat – it stated I had to give 3 month's notice. Realising that it was really inconvenient living where I was in Courbevoie – I didn't know any one and it was far out of the centre of Paris, I wrote to the agency asking them if I could leave. The response I got was that I would have to give three months, which would potentially mean spending Christmas alone. This was something that I did not want to entertain, so after speaking to Stephanie I took my contract to the hotel and asked Marcelle the bar maid what she made of it. The contract had not been signed by a third person, which she described as disgusting. After I'd written to the agency – Id been in countless times about the lack of hot water and gas, and the microwave that seemed to be promised when I moved in and which now had been taken – (in fact this microwave would not have passed Health and Safety as it sparked when you put anything which would normally be suitable to put in a microwave), I went in when my parents came to stay and with them present made up some excuse about a family bereavement. Just after we arrived at the estate agency the landlady whose flat I was renting came storming in shouting with the letter that I'd sent her (on advice from Marcelle at the hotel) giving her notice. She said to me it was not my fault, but after her hussy fit she left and I felt quite embarrassed – my parents were sat down in the agency and had obviously witnessed this too! The estate agent there asked me who had told me to write to the landlady, so I told her as I'd been advised someone I work with had. How else was I supposed to get help being 19 years old and working in a foreign country?! After the uncomfortable inventory which I was required to attend the apartment drama ended soon after and I got the majority of my deposit back after I had argued with the agency that a 3rd party should have signed the contract and that this had not been done, I wanted out. While this was going on I discussed the situation with Herbert and Stephanie, who said that I had to negotiate with the agency, which proved successful. I learnt successfully a lesson, be honest and upfront and work with other parties and ask for advice. It would have been reckless for me to have moved and stopped the direct debit from my bank account there to the agency. In fact I couldn't do this as the bank wouldn't let me. It appeared that in France there is legislation preventing direct debits from being cancelled. In any case Monsieur le Fourget the director of the agency assisted me to leave which was very much to my relief. In November of 2000 I moved out of the flat in Courbevoie – I needed a taxi to take all my belongings over to Stephanie's flat. One of the funniest moments was when I told Celine in the hotel was moving in with the two girls, she shook her head and said "Oh no!", much to the amusement of Stephanie. Stephanie had offered to accompany me been to see her landlady, Madame Legentil – she was a school headmistress and let the flat out unofficially – it was a flat that she was given due to her job in a local neighbourhood. She was in fact typically French but quite reasonable and she even confessed that she herself was apprehensive about taking on new tenants. The flat was 80 square metres and relatively quite spacious – well I had the smallest room but it was furthest from the kitchen – the walls appeared like those from Eastern Bloc flats – you could hear everything that was said from one end to the other. There was quite a comforting smell and atmosphere to the flat and the sound of the radio gave it an authentic French touch. It wasn't really any nearer to work although perhaps better connected than Courbevoie – there was a 15 minute walk to the train station where a train would take you to La Defence where you would then have to change to line 4 which takes you to Montparnasse. Line 7 went up to La Corneuve and down to Mairie d'Issy in the suburbs (banlieue) to the south. It took about 30 minutes to get to Montparnasse for work so all in all it was ok, although line 13 took me to Gaîté which was quicker. Corentin Cariou was our metro stop. The main problem with the flat was however entering and leaving. The complex was inhabited by various immigrants from Arab and West African speaking countries and they would surround the lobby, sometimes they would leave you alone, sometimes they would harass you for money or cigarettes – particularly if they had seen you go to the local tabac or if you were holding them in your hands. One several occasions I was spat upon by the son of an Arabic family and threatened with a knife – I kid you not they had a broken window when I moved in November and this had still not been fixed 11 months later. When I first started coming in and out the Arabs ran to report me to the Guardian – she knew I was a resident and told them to leave me be. "*Il faut vraiment faire attention,*" she said to me then and on a number of other occasions – I must really take care when entering and leaving. On another day the same Arab prevented me from catching my metro which I did miss – asking for money and cigarettes, I was indeed very fearful about coming in and out of the flat, even at 5.30 am in the morning. This anxiety was not something I was going to miss. Stephanie was also a victim of harassment and sexual assault in the lift – I reported this to the Guardian and she said we should call the Police. The girls did not want to do this though for fear of reprisal – that I could understand well in fairness. Stephanie was quite daring though – her bedroom looks out in to the flat courtyard and she was often kept up by a mob of youths yelling and smoking weed, so she decided to pour a bucket of water on them – the first time this was actually seen as a joke, but again it happened to her and she did the same – this was responded to by one of the mob coming up to our flat and knocking on the door, around midnight. I heard the door go and went to answer it but Stephanie pulled me back and pleaded with me not to go there. Obviously the mob had taken a dislike to her second bucket of cold water stint – Stephanie feared they may have wanted to petrol bomb the flat! Fortunately the issue did not repeat itself but it remained to be risky coming in and out. I learnt another important lesson here – let sleeping dogs lie. In this situation it is better to avoid further reprisals by being as tolerant as necessary. These were angry people, bitter at their situation in the French climate, frustrated, unemployed and bored. These were people who did not exist in real society, they had no jobs, money or prospects and were bitterly resentful of ours. The lift electrics had been smashed in on one occasion and it just seemed that we were living with people who wanted to cause trouble and upheaval.

Later on in the year there had been a petrol bombing in Crimée – the metro stop next to hours. Moreover, shortly afterwards I came home from work having worked the late shift at the hotel to find that there had been a shooting just minutes before I got home. When I got off the metro many were gathered around and I remember really feeling the tension and fear around me. The whole atmosphere around where we lived was densely populated and the environment stressful. I remember going to Monoprix once in Crimée and being literally shouted at by a supermarket assistant for taking a carrier bag without having asked for it in the first place. Walking down the street it would be hard to see anyone French! With that I mean "Français de Souche", as in someone whose roots are French and French throughout. But on the wages that we were on there was little chance of securing a property on the left bank, in the 14th, 15th or even 16th. Not denying either that where we lived was an interesting place to live, it was very dangerous at times. The Guardian herself had been beaten by one mob, so hard that she required hospital treatment on one occasion. Within the flat there was also a large room that the landlady had locked and kept us out of, however she was unaware that Julia had found a spare key so we used it to let friends stay over and for parties. When David and his sisters Leanne and Sammy came to visit, Leanne and Sammy slept in the big spare room. The French friends that came for parties were themselves frightened coming and going! I became a good friend of Aude who was a waitress but also a scholar of languages – Japanese and Russian. I was invited to her mother's flat for my birthday- this was in Belleville, 20th arrondissement. Aude had at this time a Japonese partner by the name of Hiko. He was very nice, and gentle in approach but as the couple were living with her mother they felt they needed their own space and so they decided to move out. I went after work in November and helped her do this – she wasn't moving far but was grateful for the help. Aude was very helpful about helping me improve my languages while I was in Paris and she arranged a few times to offer explanations that I hadn't understood from the course where I'd been studying a local language centre in Boulevard Raspail, 14th Arrondissement. I learnt a helpful lesson too from her – don't report someone for something that they may have done without confronting them first – this happened with a member of staff at the hotel. We had had a heated discussion as I had been dropped in it when on the buffet one evening and she hadn't offered any assistance. We had a few crossed words and then following another complaint about another worker at the next reunion I decided to bite the bullet and say how I felt! But this was another lesson learnt, the relationship between my self and this particular may not have been so frayed had I perhaps let go of the irritations I was feeling. It made me realise it is usually better to try and work things out with the person concerned first before announcing my displeasures in front of all the staff and in fact humiliating her. We did manage to sort things out though – she was very good when my brother Matt and his newly wed wife Amanda came to the restaurant on their honeymoon and gave them a 50% reduction on their bill. The Maître D'Hôtels (Head waiters and waitresses) were by and large ok – well most of the time – they were on your side. I learnt from others mistakes – from my flat mate indeed that if they were shouting at you and weren't happy, it was best to swallow your pride and graft- they didn't take kindly to you reacting to them. This wasn't always easy – but by far left me in the long term in the best position. It was a stressful environment though – expectations were high, the buffet work was relentless and at the station there was always the risk that hotel guests would leave without paying – this did not go down too well with management and lateness was really frowned upon.

The hotel although a stressful environment was a supportive environment – on several occasions I struggled emotionally to cope with the demands, training a native French guy and putting all buffet planning in. After a demanding morning one day I was shouted at by a member of staff as the chefs had been giving her some grief about the state of the buffet – something which I felt that I'd overlooked because of doing other things.

This was said in front of various other members of staff who could tell I was really upset. Straight after the lunch time meeting I went into the wash up and sobbed my heart out. I stayed here a few minutes crying thinking what the hell was I doing there. Then Thomas appeared and asked me if I was ok, followed by Celine who put her arm on me and had a mug of orange juice ready for me. I really felt they knew what I was going through and were fully supportive. Learning a job and a new language at the same time was tricky. The member of staff later appeared and we sorted things out – ready for the lunch time buffet starting at 12noon. She explained that she had been shouted at by the chefs so had felt pressured, we had a nice chat and got things back on track. She told me to look upon my time in France as a project, which I certainly did.

The FMB managers Benjamin Ladoute and Veronica Dubrois had eyes in the back of their heads could see problems a mile off – my cereal bowls were checked and hot buffet too and Benjamin in particular would ask the staff challenging questions at the daily staff gathering just before the lunch time service – he asked me where Rennes is, fortunately my Geography did not let me down and I was able to say it is in Brittany, or Bretagne as the French would pronounce. Monsieur Klosters looked very impressed on this occasion! And yes there were quite a few times when staff looked disapprovingly at my appearance from staff above myself, for my appearance – shirt hanging out, dropping a load of ice from the chilled buffet on the laminated floor creating a real hazard, sweating like a pig and also dropping an alcoholic burner for one of the heated dishes which set fire to a tea towel did not go down too well, as with the *"Arrrggh Oh Andrew"* from Veronica Dubrois on one so occasion when I picked up a big iced yoghurt bowl – that unfortunately had a massive lump of ice underneath that became unstuck and smashed onto the wooden laminated floor by the cold buffet. The heated dish incident did not cumulate in a disaster as fortunately on this occasion I was helped by guests who quickly threw ice on it so major concern were gladly avoided. I think the most annoying thing I did was when asked to man the bar was burn the milk machine and take tepid milk out to the stations *"le lait n'est pas assez chaud Andrew,"* said Rosanne breathing heavily after this announcement! Monsieur Klosters was a traditionally looking French man and I admired him greatly – he had been very kind to me and supportive, he gave me a French cuisine apron which I still have and I was sorry when he left.

I was late to work twice, the first time on my second day at work, then again in January, well and if counting the time when the Arabs on the ground floor made me miss the metro, then I was late 3 times. I was cursing these people but there was nothing that I could do or rather we could do, the three of us were all victims of this confrontation at different times. On the occasion when Stephanie was assaulted in the lift, I went to the Guardian and she advised me to tell Stephanie that she should call the Police. Both Stephanie and Julia were reluctant to do this as they feared the consequences. Who could blame them? It was a difficult environment to live in for a large proportion of the day. One day I was on the metro with Stephanie on the way home from work when a man smiling came up to us and started talking to us, it seemed harmless although in my youth I was alarmed as he seemed to be a little pushy. In my complete stupidity I told him where to go, which nearly landed me in a lot of trouble as he shouted at me *"You spoke badly, you and kicked me as I left the metro at Corentin Cariou."* When we got back to the flat Stephanie talked to me about this and said that

I'd been wreck less. *"This chap probably was living a bad life,"* she said. *"Maybe he was on drugs, or had social problems. You shouldn't have said that – he probably felt shit anyway about his life anyway, people don't need to be reminded of how bad they already feel."* I learnt an important lesson there, don't ever slate someone to their face and not expect there to be negative consequences. If you can dish out expect it back! On the day I left with my suitcases these youths were all laughing as if to say they'd succeeded in getting rid of me – I was so glad to leave. On this occasion I managed to avoid further confrontation and just walked out. As mentioned before, these were people whose life depended on drugs and cigarettes. What hope did they have to have a bright future? Then they see three individuals working, albeit on low wages but still earning a living, so obviously maybe we were easy targets. I was so glad to see the back of that area. Major lesson learnt here, maybe better to pick where I live with a view to the general area. It's no fun when living in fear every time you come home from work, or indeed when you leave early in the morning. The main poignant truth about my year in France was that while it developed me and gave me confidence, it was incredibly stressful. Living in a foreign country is pressured – everything requires more effort and not knowing where you are and what is around you and where to find things can be quite overwhelming. But I learnt to mature in France. I'd earned a proper and respectable living and had used my initiative to get out there and work. It was what I'd wanted to do and regardless of any impact it had later on with my mental health I'm extremely proud of this international living accomplishment. It also goes to show what someone lacking so much confidence can achieve given the time and space. If it taught me anything at all, aside from the other lessons it taught me to trust myself and do what I truly wanted to achieve.

Stephanie and Julia were a great support to me at work– the spoke up for me, fought my corner on occasions and were in fact my Guardian Angels. They supported me emotionally as well as practically- this was a lot easier when I was living with them. We had out rows too – in the house and at work, but we always sorted it out, and stuck together. Stephanie and I for the majority of the time having the same days off would often go out for drinks on Thursday evenings all over Paris, to République, Bastille, Champs Élysées- wherever we felt. Work colleagues invited us to parties at times and Celine's leaving do in February was at a sister hotel. The weeks seemed to fly by, every week going as follows, Saturday, Sunday and Monday the 3 of us getting the metro together, then Tuesday and Wednesday just myself and Stephanie – Julia had Tuesday and Wednesday off, as opposed to our Thursday and Friday retreat. I managed to do some travelling while living in Paris – I visited an old friend from my time when 16 at the Sue Ryder Foundation –Robert in Lyon, France's second city. Home of the unique Fourvières church and the big Part-Dieu shopping complex, there was plenty to explore-Robert's dad is of Turkish descent and owned a fast food joint in one of the suburbs of the city. While I was here I went round the city, up to the spectacular Fourvières church and around the historic centre too. Robert's dad prepared lunch for me- kebab meat and chips Coming home from Lyon I was fortunate enough to be working at the hotel in the evening. I organised other trips round France – to Reims and Epernay for champagne tasting, to St Malo, Caen, Montpellier and Bruges where I met my parents and we explored the town's attractions including a famous French tower. I enjoyed these trips out and the time out from the hotel was much appreciated.

In May I took 5 days off work to travel down to Montpellier to see French exchange partner Matthieu and his family. I'd been out to Montpellier when I was at school in lower sixth form and stayed with him, his mother Claudette, (and dad

Romain who was away at that time) brother Jerome and sister Amélie. Matthieu had replied to my letter which I sent him when I was in Courbevoie. Matthieu is actually a very caring and sincere person who I get along with very well and has excellent business acumen. He's one of those friends who you can have no contact with for months or even longer then meet and it is as if you were never apart. Typically French in outlook and looks, he has gone on to be a major success in various businesses in China where he has lived and has currently returned to France, having set up a business selling car parts in the Far East. I had a great time there with his friends although his family were in the process of moving. His dad was travelling a huge distance every weekend as he was working in La Roche Sur Yon, several hundred miles north. They had been very kind to me and we enjoyed catching up and laughing about previous times when I went to France on the school exchange- notably the night club experience at Pincho Pingo. I remember telling him though that I would be glad to return to the UK as I found the Parisian experience to be quite demanding.

The last few weeks of work came and went quickly, news spread very fast that I was planning to leave at the end of July and I enjoyed the build up to leaving although I was finally happy there in Paris, at least with housemates and work anyway I was looking forward to my plans to go to Spain. I had decided to leave to start university in September, to read French and Geography.

David, Sammy and Leanne came to visit me about a week before I was due to leave Paris. Sammy and Leanne stayed in the spare room and David in my room. I managed to take them to the Eiffel Tower and Pompidou Centre and Stephanie also gave them some tips on where to go. David and his sisters were much liked by Stephanie and Julia and we went out for drinks to various places including Place Stalingrad on one occasion. David's Mum Veronica later said how nice it was for her knowing that they were going abroad to visit me! David, Sammy and Leanne came to the hotel to have dinner and saw me in action as a waiter *"commis serveur"*. On my last day in the evening time I went with Stephanie, Julia and Andreas to the American Diner in Porte de la Villette. We had spent many happy hours in here drinking and eating and having a laugh, late after finishing work sometimes we would go down. On this occasion the mood was sombre I was due to leave in a couple of hours, it was as if there had been a death or recent funeral! Even the waitress tried to in still some warmth by smiling at us. In a way I didn't want to leave, I'd been happy with my job, earned a fair amount of holiday pay and got used to the rhythm of life there. That said, I found a lot of Parisians to be very stressed and difficult to reason with and it was tiring having to wake up so early to get to work. However, I'd made some good French friends from the hotel and I thoroughly enjoyed the freedom of being able to go anywhere in the city by metro until the early hours of the morning.

Just prior to leaving Paris I received a phone call from the local branch of my bank there to say that I had to go down to the branch as my account was in negative balance due to some transactions that had been made after I closed my account. It was a rather embarrassing situation as I thought I had completed everything and that the balance was in order. The advisor who spoke to me seemed quite perturbed that I hadn't told her that I had some outgoings not accounted for, in my defence I told her I'd given her everything she'd asked for and was unaware of any other debits. Anyway I paid up the outstanding balance and realised that in future if ever in that situation again I need be ultra careful that all transactions had been taken care of, including any cheques that had not cleared. Easy to miss but embarrassing to go through! I made sure that Stephanie learnt from this by telling her to scrutinise her receipts when closing her account.

My taxi picked me up around 8pm and I chatted to the French-Algerian taxi driver who funnily enough wanted to try and help me learn good French – a bit late for that I thought! He dropped me off with my 7 bags – to this day I cannot understand why I felt I could take this much stuff with me – I was going to Murcia, Spain, to stay with Miri's family – everyone that I across must have thought I was crazy! When I arrived at the Gare D'Austerlitz I managed to find a trolley and get on to the train with everything, with the help of some Chinese travellers who very kindly helped me onto the train. I don't know what I would have done without their help. I couldn't quite work out at this point where I was going to put all my bags given they all covered the bunker bed which I was allocated. I remember that night so well – I didn't get much sleep as I was also carrying a large amount of cash – holiday pay from the hotel. I was and am in fact a nervous traveller. I remember in the same sleeping car was a doctor from Brazil who couldn't find his ticket, and some elderly travellers. The train travelled through Orleans, down through to East of Bordeaux and beyond Toulouse. I was awoken by voices of other passengers as the train negotiated the valleys of the Pyrenees. About 30 minutes later, we arrived at the border between France and Spain, at Latour de Carol. Without much warning we had to get off the train and wait for the Spanish sprinter service into Barcelona. Lugging 7 bags was not the easiest task, given that there were no trolleys at this remote station. When I got on the Spanish train the border control police came on and demanded to see passports – but where the hell was mine?!! I couldn't find it! I searched through of my bags and eventually found it, the police man advising me to keep it closer to me in future. For all you travellers out there remember learn from me! Always keep your passport and travel documents close to hand! The train wended its way through the hillside towns descending into the Catalonian plain – the whole journey took around 3 hours, and as we neared to Barcelona we picked up commuters from the surrounding suburbs. On arrival in Barcelona once again gathering my year load of belongings from Paris I went to change some money and enquire about a train to Murcia, where fortunately I managed to get a fairly cheap seat in 1st class as there were no 2nd class tickets now available. The whole journey only cost an incredible £35, bearing in mind the Spanish currency was still the Peseta at this time. The journey on board the Talgo bound for Murcia (destination Cartagena) was very comfortable and I sat back and relaxed, going to the bar for a drink or cigarette. After having to change carriages in Alicante, the train arrived on time in Murcia where I was greeted by Miri and her brother Pablo. What a relief that was after a frantic night and day of travelling with my 7 bags of possessions from Paris.

I spent a week with Miri's family – (parents Carmen and Pascual, also her sisters Nuria and Sonia) spent by their pool, in los Vientos which is close to the town of Molina De Segura, and also with Pablo by the beach with his friends, drinking and taking in the Spanish sun. It felt great here, a bit like paradise, being very hot and sunny, and a beautiful view - I could relax, sleep and take in the amazing Spanish lifestyle.

Chapter 3

DIAGNOSIS AT UNIVERSITY

My holiday was short lived however when I arrived home, with my 7 bags! After I'd been at home a few days I decided to get a job in a local hotel, this so happened to be the same venue where my sister got married in 2007. My place at university had been deferred as happily Id been told in November 1999 that my French A level had been remarked and awarded a grade 'B' instead of the previous 'C' which I was really pleased about.

When I started university I was unusually quite confident – but I put this down to my French experience which had been a major success. My dad (pops) took me down to university in the car – it felt a bit surreal if honest. That said he took me down and when we'd unpacked everything had lunch, some beef and mustard sandwiches. That evening I met my hall mates and Sarah, the floor tutor who went through some housekeeping rules, notably keeping the music down at night. It was quite awkward making new friends and I strived to find things in common with people. However I met some really nice funny people and started to settle in. Fresher week came and went and I got into the swing of things with my course, I was reading

French and Geography. About 10 days into term I had my birthday and went out drinking with my floor mates. I guess I was happy to have made new friends and with how things were going, until I had some terrible news- my grandma sadly passed away after suffering pneumonia. I remember the funeral and how sudden it came and went. Coming back to university I became unusually hyper and I started to sleep less and less. Around the end of October I started to stay out late at night and get taxis to my friend Sebastien's house, often taking drink with me. In university I contributed to lectures more and more and knew the answers to more and more difficult scenarios. I led team work and fellow students commented on how much I knew. This is where the mania started.

Sebastien was at this time an acquaintance/friend, French and so happened to originate from Paris. When my mood started to become slightly elated he invited me to a party where I was extremely chatty and sociable. We got a long well and I got invited out to more and more Erasmus parties. However I started to take more and more risks, yet I had started to develop hyper sensitivity – Id been at a party with Sebastien and been overly concerned about the health and safety of having so many people in such a small house. I was sensationalised by the claustrophobia, rooted through tens of coats and went out side feeling the need to protect us both from this awful unsafe environment. When Sebastien came out looking for me I gave him his coat and walked off. I was starting to experience psychosis now thinking I could see who was evil and who was good. The next night, I left my hall of residence late at night to have a deep and meaningful conversation with him at 3am in the morning. On this night I got a taxi and had an argument with the taxi driver as he had taken me to the wrong Rectory road address. On a previous occasion with my hall mates we had complained about the cost of the taxi and told the taxi driver we would only give him £5, I thought it would be good to be so assertive like this, but on this occasion I was alone and very vulnerable. *"This isn't the Rectory road that I know,"* I said. I started complaining at the taxi driver who reluctantly took me to the address I wanted to go to. I then slammed some money down, saying *"that's all I've got."* When I arrived at Sebastien's house I banged on the door, it was now 3.10am and ran off to find Sebastien's house. Sebastien opened the door. He looked a bit shocked not surprisingly to see me, and said was I aware of the time. We sat and chatted, although the chat started with him asking me what the hell I was doing coming round at 3am! I was chatting freely and I felt as though I was becoming something that I wasn't sure of. To this day I cannot remember what I had been saying. *"Maybe you're just too mature for your age,"* Sebastien said. I'd recently taken on a floor rep responsibility and had included a fire evacuation which I had felt disappointed – to me no-one seemed interested in my efforts although I'd taken things a bit too seriously. I also had gone to great extremes to organise a party with pizza. Along with my course and efforts to please everybody, I had been heading towards trouble. Mixed in with that had been the death of my grandma in late October who I miss so much to this day. I was becoming more and more emotionally unstable and felt very confused.

Indeed, when Peter came to see me the day before I was admitted to the QE. The day before, I had felt "on top of the world", so elated, I felt that amazing things were going to happen, friends were going to organise surprise parties on barges – I felt I had become a new invincible person, able survive without sleep and without the need to eat and able to have sexual contact all day and night. I had felt absolutely amazing. I had asked Peter if Leon was dead. Mum had explained previously that Leon had not been looking after himself at university, he'd not been eating. Peter, had just said *"No, he was not dead."* We had met at the central station and I appeared to him very drowsy and confused. At the station there was a sales man selling a Virgin credit card. Using my special powers (in my head) that I had developed over the last few days I could see right through him and realised he was just after my money. We went on to eat at Mcdonalds where I appeared so tired that I could hardly eat my burger. Peter seemed to be staring back at people who were watching me. We went back to my room but I was so tired I could hardly keep my eyes open walking back to my hall of residence. When we got back I told Peter about my hallucinations and everything I'd experienced that day. I told him how high Id been on campus then within 30 minutes how I crashed and could not keep my eyes open. and how on that day too just before meeting Peter, after two nights of not sleeping, and having walked to Sebastian's house in the early hours of Saturday morning, I had stopped up in my room playing music and felt great, full of energy. I continued by telling Peter that I had decided to walk to Sebastian's again, feeling like I could rule the world. I arrived at 7.30am, banged on the door, Sandrine Sebastian's fellow French housemate answered. *"I'm sorry Andrew Sebastien is sleeping."* I can't to this day say what else she said, but I remember the fatigue coming on a few hours later after I started to hallucinate that my flat mates had organised a party for me on a barge and how it was now raining, and I'd walked to the library. The security guard had taken one look at me and ushered me into the staff room. I started talking and talking and staring constantly at the security guard whose colleague then came in and then walked off after they could not get a word in edge ways. I wasn't not sure to this day if they were going to get help but I left immediately afterwards and started hearing voices of people cheering, saying *"Andy, Andy!"* I thought, *"Oh great, they've organised something really special for me, I'm so lucky to have such nice friends!"* But when I arrived at the station next to the canal, there was no barge there. When I walked to the station, I started to hallucinate again. The trains that passed at the station seemed to go straight through me, and when a train came (literally it seemed just a minute after the express trains had passed) I got on, and started to see people as 'figures'. By this stage I was so tired I was falling asleep. After I'd met up with Peter and got back to my room he left and I fell into a deep sleep. My hall mates had cooked me a meal when I awoke on the night before I was admitted to hospital- when I entered the kitchen it seemed they were all looking at me- I felt paranoid as they all appeared to be in on some sort of conspiracy against me and I felt really confused and distressed and they called for the hall porter who came to my room, we had a nice chat and he was an extremely caring guy, although the severity of how ill I was had not been yet apparent.

That night when I awoke I went completely manic, listened to music until I started to shake. I was uncontrollable and became terrified of my situation. I cling on to the fact that I knew I was unwell but could not control my distressed state screaming down the corridor. There was no floor tutor there as Sarah was away. My flat mates were completely frightened and told me to go get some help, I ran down to the security office and rang the bell continuously for 5 minutes, and still no one came. I went back to my room, and I rang Monica, one of mum's best friends. My phone battery was nearly dead, but we had a brief chat and she told me to drink some water and take some deep breaths. She was calm and reassuring and told me I had just not been feeling myself. We agreed that I should call the security number and they arranged for a tutor to come to me. He was a lovely calm Chinese PhD student, and when he came I rang Monica again and she spoke with him and he stayed with me for several hours and then I was looked after by an amazing Spanish Porter who comforted me and gave me cigarettes. I was completely unwell now, threatening all sorts of things, mostly about my parents which were particularly distressing for them. I was absolutely adamant I would not see them. The

Porter asked me if I had any siblings and I immediately said, yes my sister Jackie who had at this time a boyfriend Channa. They came straight away from London, but before they arrived a doctor arrived who wanted to give me some medication which I refused. A member of staff from the hall of residence asked if I'd like it if he sat in on this GP consultation. It seemed that once I'd refused the medication the GP just seemed to shrug his shoulders and leave. Now this was to my advantage, as Jackie said, it was the right thing to do as I needed to be properly assessed. I spent some time with a lovely floor tutor but was hallucinating and seeing things that were not there. When you hallucinate, your brain is not filtering out the rubbish. I was seeing many different things, having many thoughts and emotions all mixed up. I thought I could read people's minds, see whether people were really genuine or fake, while yet within a very short time span I was worrying unnecessarily about things that were out of my control, angry at my parents, terrified of them too, elated at the thought my friends were supposedly organising a party for me, while yet I thought terrible things had happened to people I knew. Alex from when I was working as a waiter in Paris I believed had been poisoned by her parents but had escaped to freedom…I thought that another friend, Georgina had been locked up by her parents and was chained up. I rang Georgina's mum and accused her of mistreating her children that morning. She realised quickly that I wasn't well- well it must have been a big shock to her. I was shouting by this point, screaming that I would have my parents arrested for harassment if they came near me. I rang Monica again and she told me that they had promised me they would not come. These few hours seemed like a lifetime. Shortly later I was assessed by another doctor who said that I should be taken to the local hospital (QE) as a matter of urgency. Channa came with me to my room and got an overnight bag and we went out to the car, following the member of staff whose car we followed to the hospital. We were waiting a while in the waiting area at what

appeared to be a deserted reception area of the hospital. It was after all Sunday night there were few staff around. I remember getting restless and Jackie encouraged me to sit down and eat some food. Initially I resisted and then came Yasin, a lovely guy who was also suffering a psychiatric breakdown and was already an inpatient. He lit up a cigarette in the reception area (bearing in mind it was strictly no smoking!) and asked me if I'd like to join him. I said yes straight away and in spite of the prohibition I insisted on smoking with Yasin. He was my best friend in the hospital and he said this to me straight away. After we had smoked Yasin left and a lady who I believe was a CPN came and I became very emotional, telling her that she had no idea what I was going through and didn't understand. It seemed to me that I thought I'd made her cry. *"We do try to understand,* "she said, seeming to have tears in her eyes. Shortly afterwards an on call psychiatrist arrived. His name was Dr Crawley and he looked and appeared to be acting to me like a robot. He never seemed to stop staring at me. So, angry and frustrated at him I stared back. He took me into a side room and I told him that I had completed an assessment of him and said he looked ill not me. I maintained that I felt fine and that there had been some funny mistake. *"You'll not get me staying in a loony bin like this,"* I said. *"You're not well and need help."* The assessment did not last long and after then I went back out and told Jackie and Channa what had happened. I was starting however to get very tired and so they took me into a side room where there was a sofa. An Approved Mental Health Professional arrived and she encouraged me to try and sleep. *"You do look exhausted, Andrew"* she said.
"I just want everything to return to normal, I don't want to die."
"It will do, Andrew," she replied.
The next few days were a blur – a mist of hallucinations and drifting in and out of consciousness. Once on the ward, I was still held in disbelief that I needed to be there. Shortly after my voluntary admission I remember being sat with my bag and

saying that I thought it was a mistake being admitted to hospital, *"So I'm in the loony bin, oh I don't need to be here." "This is a hospital for sick people, this is not a loony bin"*, replied the nurse. I continued to hear voices and believing that cars were slowing outside to see him. I remembered my old friend Paul, believing that I'd seen his dad drive slowly past the lounge window of the ward staring at me in a threatening way. I also was absolutely fearful of my room in the hospital, that there was a hit man hiding above the ceiling. My mum had told me that before being admitted that Leon had not been eating at university and his parents had been very concerned about him. In my misguided mind I thought that certain people were also being abused by his father. I continued to refuse to see my parents, and when they did come, I threw back any gifts they had for me back in their faces. On one occasion I ripped up a bar of chocolate. *"Pick that up,"* ordered a nurse. Because the nurse had told me to pick it up, I did. I wanted to show them they could not control me. I wanted to torment them that I would listen to the nurse but not them in passive aggressive manner. Indeed of course that was not their intention. Following this my psychosis took a turn for the worse, where I thought staff were deliberately keeping me in hospital by putting tablets into food in the restaurant. At one point I refused to eat as I thought this was a trap. I feared that the cleaning member of staff was also conspiring against me, spraying the toilets so much with air freshener that they wanted to intoxicate me. This terrifying experience carried on with the absolute fear that staff were trying to kill me. There were three male nurses that worked at the weekend which I had made myself believe that I could not stand. You see, in this environment, I felt that I could read into people and make judgements and evaluations as to whether they were genuine or fake, to be trusted or not to be trusted. And these three nurses I definitely did not trust. So on the Friday night when I believed they were going to kill me when I heard them rub their hands together and say *"We're going to have some fun this weekend"*. I have never been more petrified. So I packed my bag and, when I was ready, I ran down the corridor and out of ward 3. By this time they were running after me, I kept going. Adrenaline pumping I made it to the last set of doors. However my relief was to be short lived as the ward door leading to the main reception had been locked. Then they caught up with me, they were very cross with me, I felt so terribly afraid about what they were going to do with me, so I pressed the fire alarm. The nurses carried me down, where they restrained me and injected me with diazepam, and put me on an immediate temporary section. I remember speaking to the ward manager but as I was given a strong tranquiliser I do not remember anything else. Following this terrifying experience I had to be escorted to and from the canteen. There was a male nurse who I really did not like who came to me one day and told me he was going to take me to the post office as there was a postal order from my parents. I felt so scared with this nurse, I really didn't trust him. I thought the whole way he was planning to have me done over and I felt so tense on the way home when I thought he was going to grab me that I screamed *"Don't touch me"* and the nurse told me as a result of this I had really let him down and destroyed my chances of getting discharged soon. Of course this is what I thought I heard as I was still very poorly and the nurse concerned was only doing his job. In my distressed state I felt so much relief when we arrived at the hospital entrance and back onto the ward. I honestly thought I wasn't going to get back alive.

One of my room mates Ellis was admitted with a mental health problem also. At first we seemed to get along but then he moved rooms due a change around of beds and went onto another ward so I didn't get to see him after this. Ali, on the other hand remained in the room next to mine and was a kind hearted Pakistani guy who had his own health concerns but was incredibly supportive towards me. He had severe depression but really looked out for me. He would call me into his room after we had been called to have out medication and would offer me popcorn. When we were in the smoking room, he would always ask me how I was feeling and I would do the same for him. One of the few regrets I have ever had is not keeping in touch with him, and also a girl called Millie. Millie was a really supportive friend and I found a nice sense of humour in her and soon after we had met we would quite often sit smoking or playing games. She was quite a motivator for me to build my confidence up by keeping busy. She used to call me *"chicken,"* when I did not have the guts to ask the nurse on duty if I could leave the ward for half an hour. Millie and Ali would comfort me when I was really lo, on one occasion I was too distressed to pluck up the courage to go to the canteen. Katie one of the nurses saw this and got me a sandwich, and Millie and Ali helped calm me down and later we watched Jurassic Park. Towards the end of my stay Pops (my father) came to visit alone and Millie said *"Come on Andrew lets get your dad a cup of tea."* She was really kind like that. Whilst out with Pops (don't ask me how I managed this) but I managed to persuade him to buy me and Millie a pack of cigarettes each, much to Millie's surprise yet delight too. Pops had given me the parental lecture about smoking and said he didn't at all condone smoking. Yet I needed them yet as while I needed to be admitted it was sheer torture at the same time. There were not enough things to do and smoking seemed to take up just a small proportion of the time. Millie and I were and are alike, sensitive people who during that time could tell who we liked and trusted. One of the nurses at this time in my mind that was against me was Isabel, one of the nurses it seemed would spoil any nice activity or be deliberately awkward. She would break up happy conversations between Yasin and myself, but she was someone who I tormented when ill so she had a lot to put up with when all said and done! While in hospital I realised I may be stuck there for a long time so I said to the nurses that

I needed a solicitor. A Mental health solicitor was called from a neighbouring town, she was really nice and told me that she was going to help me apply to get me off a section. Once off the section I would be free to leave the hospital if I so wished. That night I was asked to see a Dr Greenfield. I'd previously been feeling quite upbeat. However when I saw Dr Greenfield she started to interrogate me and make me doubt myself. In the end I left the room really upset yet angry. She was trying to see how much questioning I could take, although at the time it felt like she was deliberately trying to trip me up just before my Mental Health Tribunal. The Mental Health Tribunal took place the following day just after lunch. I remember the lay person leading the tribunal being quite openly critical towards the psychiatrist who arrived late. The psychiatrist argued that I would not be able to cope with stressful situations outside of the hospital. Being unwell but not realising, I accused Dr Holden and Dr Greenfield of deliberately holding me there against my own free will and that they were the only people in the room who wanted to keep me locked up. My Mum and Pops were there along with the Mental Health Solicitor and Tracey, one of the nurses. Mum and Pops said when asked to comment said they wanted to listen to what the doctors and nurses thought were best for me. After all, they did know best. Having a Section 2 order withdrawn perhaps would have felt like a victory, if it had happened for me in the short term, but would it have been so in the long run? What if I'd become unwell again out of hospital because my mood had not settled and I was not therefore coping well with day to day situations? Things may well have escalated and I may have had to have gone back into hospital. Now that would not have been good. So in spite of my pig headedness the Section 2 order remained as the panel were in agreement that it was in my best interests that I stayed in hospital until I was recovering to a stage that I would be well enough to be back in the community. They had increased my Olanzapine from 10mg at night to 10mg in the morning as well and this slowed down my metabolism, causing me to put on weight. This helped to stabilise my mood and reduced the psychosis and hallucinations. However I had lost all my confidence and self esteem and feared interacting with others. When the doctors said I was fit to go on home leave, I remember I had absolutely nothing to say to anyone. Pops picked me up and took me home and the drive home was in silence. Back home I found it a bit easier to talk and I chatted to them about what had gone on when in the hospital.

Mum and June took me back to hospital after being home for the weekend. June and Monica are two of Mum's best friends. I remember when we got back to ward 3 Mum talked to Charlie while June talked to me. It was really a lovely gesture of June to support Mum and Pops in this way. I stayed back in hospital for a further 4 nights when it was ward round and one of the doctors, a lovely Indian doctor said that I could go home on home leave for a week with a view to being discharged. Pops picked me up for this. The following Thursday mum took me down to the QE where I went to be officially discharged. When we left the hospital and went up to the University and went to the canteen I remember feeling very unconfident at asking the member of staff for what I required. I found the simplest of things too stressful, like being in a car or walking into a pub for several months after discharge. I felt very isolated and socially excluded and that everyone was staring at me – some sort of paranoia. I tried to go back to university after Christmas, yet I realised quickly with Mum and Pop's support that it was way too soon to think about going back. One day when back at home in January 2001 I felt so low I was crying continuously and Mum came home and took me straight to the doctors. The doctor referred me to Community Mental Health and I saw Layla Hunter CPN, a lovely lady who came out to see me. I remember Layla telling me when I told her how low I felt, she told me that I had to challenge the negative thoughts.

Instead of catastrophising she advised me to do a range of activities, meeting friends, exercise, activities when at home. I saw Layla every 2 weeks up until the summer of 2001 when she discharged me as I was making excellent progress and due to start university again in September. Layla was the first CPN I saw in the community apart from a brief spell when but she was a great support, not just to me but to my family too. I told her how meeting people was in fact a chore, and how I had no idea how to make conversation or know what to say. Layla explained that this was normal given I had been in hospital for nearly a month. She empathised and encouraged me to reintroduce new activities and exercise. Mum and Pops felt that doing a job would do me the world of good – something to focus on, keep me busy and have an achievement at the end of it. I feared this greatly and when I started at a local hotel, I was a nightmare to work with! I struggled to take instructions, was disorganised and slow. But I had some good colleagues who helped me. Sylvia was really supportive and I was put at ease by her. Bit by bit I made progress to the satisfaction of the Restaurant Manager and in June 2001 I left to do my ECDL computer course. It was a great feeling to know that Id held a job down for 4 months and got some money to show for it.

After a two week holiday at Matt and Amanda's in Arborfield I met up with Jane, Jessica and Rebecca, this helped me to find my feet and meet up with some friendly faces. I went with Amanda to London three times and twice with Matt and I found this break really helped me to feel better. I felt happy knowing that I was going back to university, but did I still want to do the same course? Since meeting Miri and her family several years ago I yearned to speak Spanish. So I contacted the admissions department at my chosen university for Hispanic Studies and successfully switched from French and Geography to French and Hispanic Studies.

Chapter 4

RETURN TO UNIVERSITY

I started back at University in September 2001 and got my place of residence secured at a local Hall. It was in the same hall of residence where I had stayed the year before when diagnosed. Nestled in a wooded park with a lake, it was actually quite a tranquil place to live. I arranged an appointment with Dr Belfringham my GP for the first time and she was very welcoming – smiling when she first saw me. Dr Belfringham was obviously fully aware of what had happened the year before from my medical notes and throughout my time at university she kept a very close eye on me.

I was happy also that Dr Belfringham arranged for me to see Eve Shinney CPN (Community Psychiatric Nurse) who I had really liked and got on very well with. Eve had been on ward 3 where I had been staying. During the majority of the first year I used to go and walk over to see her at the Community Mental Health Centre there- I used to talk about how university was going, and I remember Eve saying that she was very happy to see me back at university following an extremely turbulent and traumatic time in my life. We got on extremely well and we talked a lot about coping strategies and activities that I could do in the evenings. She also kept a close eye one me, and the medication I was on however was working and I was coping well with my new course, French and Spanish. I struggled with Spanish and my marks were low but I attended every class and received some extra help from Alexandra, the Spanish languages tutor. At the end of the year I passed all my exams – I just needed to pass anyway in the first year. When I saw my personal tutor Dr Walters he told me that I had been put forward for the Joseph Manson memorial prize for outstanding achievement! That was because of my efforts to pass Spanish. So I was very happy- Dr Belfringham, who was by far the best doctor I have ever had, congratulated me too. She would insist on seeing me every week and she was not only a GP but also a psychiatrist and support worker rolled into one in my eyes. She did after all know how seriously unwell I had been the previous year.

My grades in my first year were better in French than in Spanish – in fact by two classifications but I had been determined to pass in Spanish. I had made some more friends in my hall and had enjoyed going out and socialising again. The first year had been fairly eventful too as one night after a night out in the city centre I decided stupidly to walk home at about 1am only to be chased towards the nearest hall of residence by some thugs who cornered me into a closed co-educational building and threatened me with a knife, taking my wallet and phone. I ended up telling them my pin number although I later ascertained no money had been taken. I had run like mad towards the Chamberlain tower, I banged on the door and screaming that I've been mugged. The security guard let me in and arranged for a car to take me down to the Hall of Residence, where I was living. I spent half the night speaking to the Police, and I ended up phoning up my part time employer, a telesales company explaining what had happened and that I would not be in work the next day. The next day I remember feeling threatened and anxious, that someone was going to pull a knife on me. It took a while to get over that experience and I was much more cautious as a result. As per the hall of residence secretary who gave me a stern few words on looking after myself, I decided walking back at 1am from a night out just because I wanted to save a fiver was probably in the balance of things a risk not worth taking in future. I will never forget though the ridiculous phone my parents let me following the mugging and my rogue of a friend (!) Jeremy knew I could not work out how to put it on silent so he insisted on ringing me when in French Lectures... and not just any lecture, but Bernadette Sentier's lecture on French language!

Yes I was definitely achieving things again, as stated previously I was working part time as a telesales advisor in the nearby city centre on a Wednesday afternoon and Saturday morning, I was enjoying my course and making new friends. How had I made this happen? I guess I made the move to go back to university because I'd been making small steps i.e. the hotel job, doing exercise, doing a course i.e. having a routine, meeting with friends, accessing support, being compliant with medication. All these things together made one big positive statement that I was getting better and moving on with my life.

During the first year one day, my friend Cheryl said that she had caught wind that I had an admirer, by the name of Billie, a girl who was in the post A level Spanish group. I was flattered! But the reality was that I knew it wouldn't go anywhere. Anyway I agreed to go on a date with her, she was lovely, friendly and easy to get on with. But I just didn't feel anything. I think I tried to force myself to like her to please her. Anyway there was no romance and although there was no romance we did sort things out. That summer I went to stay with my friend Selina who I'd met via a friend at my hall of residence. Selina had come to stay for the weekend and I will never forget how again I was put in a compromising position... Selina thought I liked her and a friend from home, Dan decided it would be a good idea to say what a nice couple we would make… which prompted her to come into my bedroom telling me what he's said… I could have died!

But that summer I did some travelling and had a nice time at Selina's parents in Normandy. We did a bit of local sight seeing and went to Honfleur and Monet's garden at Giverny. I then went on to visit Morlaix, St Malo and then went on to see Sebastian the French guy who I met in the autumn of 2000 just prior to becoming unwell. I finally travelled over night to Munich from Paris and stayed with Stephanie (who I'd shared the apartment with in Paris), and met her parents and stayed in her swanky Schwabing apartment. I was however quite glad to be out of her car particularly as she did in excess of 120 mph on the German Autobahn. Stephanie had always been brutally honest with me about my weight, maybe this was her German nature, but she had seen a different Andrew: before diagnosis I was a slim, young looking slightly immature guy. Well I did smoke before becoming ill, I guess the fact that I also liked my cakes and chocolate added to the unhealthiest type of lifestyle that astounded Wendy! So she had me on a diet and got me jogging, that being when we later went from Munich to the Black Forest where we stayed with her parents. It was for sure that at this point she recognised things that I had not seen.

While I was out gallivanting in Europe, I had sub-let my room (in the house I had decided to live in with 4 housemates) to Matthieu my French exchange partner as he needed somewhere to live over the summer as he was going to be doing an internship at a local night club. When I came back from my holidays I spent the remainder of the time working at home in a factory and commuting to see Matthieu and the girls I was going to live with. It had been a great summer, Matthieu had settled in well and despite a few tensions he got on well with my housemates and he organised a barbeque that was a night to remember. Karin, one of the girls and I were particularly sad to see Matthieu leave and his departure was particularly difficult – more difficult for us than for him, given that we were left in a big house that had been a hive of activity over the summer. Matthieu had organised a barbecue towards the end of his stay with people from his place of work over the summer and also us housemates – I had been working at home to earn some money and coming down to the house mid week and at weekends to visit. It was really sad to see him leave and we all missed him around the house, but we had all had an amazing summer and it had been a pleasure to have been able to have him rent out my room.

The second year came quickly at university and I seemed to make good ground and improve my grades. I got employment at House of Fraser as a sales assistant which helped me out financially, until I got to the point where I had reduced my hours as much as possible so I decided towards the end of the academic year to give it up. I had enjoyed working with the other team members, on the bed linen and towels departments but the pressure of exams took over. Dr Belfringham, was as ever extremely supportive at all times and continued to see me every week. The second year counted for a only small percentage of our overall grade but even so it was important to remain focused and do my very best.

My summer as a key camp courier started off great; I took the train to the Vendée and met Matthieu and his family in La Roche Sur Yon. We spent a few days at the beach, and at the casino, and some good time catching up! Matthieu had not changed a bit since the last time we'd met when he came to stay- typically Mediterranean in looks, dark, and slender... still with a great sense of humour and open too. One night I remember we were sat in his parent's lounge talking and it was

then I first became fully aware that I had feelings for blokes. But here was a guy who knew my sexuality already and tried really hard to coax it out of me. But I wasn't ready to come out. I was so far in denial I couldn't begin to admit, again, this was the case a few days later on the last night when in Bordeaux Matthieu said to me,
"You know Andrew I have always asked myself if you are gay". "I'm not," I replied rather defensively. *"I just havn't met the right woman".* "Ok," Christophe replied, *"I'm sure that you will get married to a nice lady and be very happy."* I was in denial here and I knew it big time.

The time in Bordeaux was great with Matthieu, we'd been out meeting some relatives of his, had barbecues and met various friends too. However my time in Bordeaux was quite brief as a result of my commitment to work for Key camp near Tours. I'd agreed with Matthieu that if he wanted to, he could meet me at the camp site later on in the summer. On the last night in Bordeaux we had stayed up until 5am talking and oblivious that we may overlay I woke to find my train had left 10 minutes beforehand. Panic overcame me and we both got up straightaway! I left Matthieu in a hurry at Bordeaux train station having frantically phoned to the camp site to explain I had overslept, apologising profusely that I would be on the next train to Tours!

On arrival in Tours I was picked up by the assistant area manager who took me to the campsite where I would do my training. The next few days were spent meeting other reps and before I knew it I had been placed with another girl, Vicky at the St Clémence campsite. The first and second night were spent in a caravan that I shared with Vicky, a slim blonde haired Manchurian. The weather had been extremely hot and on the first night in a tent it suddenly became windy, but not just windy but a fierce tornado which whipped up around the campsite and up lifted tents, blew trees down and scared a Dutch family so much that they came into the key camp staff quarter with screaming frightened children. But word soon came of a tent that been uprooted, which hadn't been pegged down. It was Kelly's tent and several of us were drafted to salvage what was left of Kelly's belongings. As we ran up in the sheer torrential rain with thunder and lightning it felt like we were the heroes of an action adventure moving, coming to the rescue to save the day. I basically did as I was told! When I went back to our tent, completely drenched and clothes sodden, I lent the Dutch family an already sodden towel. Around one hour later there was calm as the storm settled down.

The next day I was woken around 7am by a customer, clearly shocked by what had happened. A tree trunk had fallen flat on top of several cars. Matt, a tall friendly guy who I shared a tent with me awoke just after I did and reassured *"It's alright Andy I'll come with you"*. The man was clearly distressed and wanted solutions, which unfortunately we were not able to give him. During the storm families had left the campsite in droves to seek refuge elsewhere. One person in the region on another campsite was killed. My first night in a key camp tent had been memorable.

When the hype regarding the storm was over, the campsite cleared up and everything was back to normal, key camp duties resumed and I was paired up with Matt. I was actually sharing a tent with him and didn't really get to know him on my infamous first night in the tent. Matt was to be my main ally and supporter throughout my time on the campsite. The first contact with Matt was when I was changing a gas bottle and making rather a pig's ear of it. I think at the time I thought, *"He must think I'm a real idiot"*. But in fact Matt and I got on like a house on fire. We got on really well and he really looked out for me. One morning after collecting the cleaning bucket he said, *"We should be bat man and robin*", and so from that moment onwards we were just that – guess who was Robin?! We had loads of fun, raced down tracks on the campsite, ate breakfast on customer's tables, and had spray bottle fights with Steve, John and Sam. At the end of the clean we would always have a race and then in the afternoons, as I was still a bit shy with others, Matt would include me in group activities in the swimming pool and the 'hot tub'. It was really turning into a great working stay and I had certainly made a really great friend in him.

Throughout my time on the camp site I had remained very "closed" to others about having some sort of feelings that others would describe as quite gay. I remember wanting to tie a colleague Sharon's hair together and this feisty Scottish Canvass worker accused me of being gay to which I denied, rather abruptly, being defensive- which looking back is often a sign that the other person is right… yes I was in denial, petrified of what others would think of me. I forced myself to like women, I even dated Josephine, the French bar maid which did not work out, surprise surprise. All because I wanted to save face!

One day we were larking about as usual – well we were cleaning out a customer's tent and I was asked to go with a customer in his car to the local village. There had been a serious car accident involving an English family and a French lorry and I had been asked to translate. When we got there the scene was carnage, there were several ambulances there I was immediately briefed by a fellow English holiday maker. The parents were more seriously injured than the children, and following a few intense efforts in the ambulances translating names, addresses, dates of birth, and going into the ambulance of the father and translating for the doctor and father English – French –English I was released from duty. I just remember feeling extremely shaky, so much so that the firemen "Pompiers" saw me crouching on the grass and came to see if I was ok.

Pete, the area manager asked me if I'd be prepared to go back the hospital to visit the family and assist with translating for the family. I went with Pete to the adult hospital in Tours where Pat got out to assist with translating for the boy's mother and father. Pete then took me onto the children's hospital in Tours. I remember at the time being told that the family were very lucky, Tours is one of few relatively small cities in France that has a specialist children's hospital, and an excellent one at that. On arrival myself and Pete were shown to the room where the boys were still unconscious. The doctor explained to me, that while they hadn't suffered any major injuries, they had suffered significant trauma. After talking to the boys, Scott and Joseph, we stayed with them and I was able to translate for the boys and doctor's benefit.

After a long day at the hospital I came home, via the adult hospital to pick up Pat. We were all exhausted and very hungry and so we called at Mcdonald's on the way home. I don't think that Pat had anything to say to me, although the experience seemed to have given us some sort of bond.

I was extremely pleased to find out that the family who had the terrible car accident all made a full recovery, the mother and boys came back to stay at the campsite for about a week while the boy's father remained in hospital. The boys gave inflatables, tennis rackets, footballs amongst other things as a way of a big thank you us, which was really touching.

My friendship continued to flourish with Matt. Matt was such a sound ally who never challenged me about my sexuality and I often moaned to him about some of the rumours that were flying around. As the summer unfolded, Fiona left the campsite and Matt's attention went onto another girl. I tried to be a good friend to them both and we often sat in our tent smoking and drinking and just talking. Unfortunately this friendship was met

Andrew Spriggs

with an abrupt end when Matt became involved in a fracas with a holiday maker. It appeared that a group of the camp lot had gone into the village, come back and had, continuing to drink heavily, caused a lot of noise. As a consequence the holiday makers complained to the owner of the campsite who ordered that two members of the courier team were to be offsite by the end of the next day. I had been unaware of the incident due to being completely run down with a virus. As the day unfolded and in spite of attempts by the holiday makers who clearly felt that the apology given had been enough and tried to retract the complaint, the owner insisted that a member of each camp were to leave to site. So Mateos, the Dutch courier volunteered to leave. I was gutted; my best mate on the campsite had been kicked off - so much seemed to have happened over these last few months.

Towards the end of the season, my good friend Matthieu came to stay and we shared a caravan. We did in fact have a lot of fun, spent a day at Chinon at the chateau then we invited all the keycamp round, so there again having lots of fun, smoking and drinking, playing games and of course upsetting one or two neighbours with the level of noise! We went to the local club which was a little reminder of Pincho Pingo back in Montpellier....plenty of women... again I was upset – I believe because I did not feel truly happy. Matthieu realised this, and being the good friend he is spent a lot of time comforting me... At the time he thought that I was upset due to issues from the past, I was however looking back trapped as I felt I could not be myself.

Soon after Matthieu left the camp site custom started to wind up, the shop closed and the number of holiday makers started to dwindle. We were allowed to move into caravans and had many parties and drinking games – it was a real laugh and I enjoyed having a bit of space to myself. Matthieu left the campsite to prepare for his Erasmus year in Sheffield the following academic year.

The last day came at St Catherine de Fier Bois and we all completed the season, bar Matt and Mateos, successfully. On returning Nadine had asked me if I would like to stay at her mum's given the flight from Tours arrived back into Stansted airport very late, along with Hannah and of course Steve as well. Steve had become a good friend, I'd been fishing with him at St Catherine lake, and got to know him better on nights out on the campsite.

After leaving Steve and Nadine at her mother's home, Nadine's mum took us to Stansted airport as she was due to be attending court near to Stansted, Hannah got her flight back to Newcastle, and I got the train to Birmingham. Pops had spoken to me a few days before leaving St Catherine to tell me that Matthew (my step brother) had had a serious motor bike accident and had had to be airlifted to hospital in Birmingham. A fairly distant friend picked me up at New Street station and I spent a night in her flat. The next day I visited Matthew who told me that he couldn't wait to get out of hospital, that it was really a crap situation to be in and how frustrated he was not to be able to get up and go out and about. After a good chat I left, went home to Chesterfield and met Matthieu once again albeit briefly in Sheffield —he was embarking on an Erasmus year there as part of his Business degree- it was a real shame that I was now to embark on a year in Spain while one of my oldest friends was going to be just 10 miles from my home town! Still a big smoker at this point, I puffed away as he announced that he had made a pact with friends to stop and that he was trying to stick to it. While it was nice to see him, it had been strange to see him on 3 separate occasions that year, twice in France, at La Roche, St Clémence and now in Sheffield. We said our good byes and I came home to The Gables and packed for my next adventure: I was going to live and study in Murcia, Spain. I'd learnt an awful lot out in France and gained some invaluable experience on the campsite, dealing with customers, emergencies and also using my language skills. It had also improved my confidence.

The departure to Murcia was imminent following my visit to see my brother and Matthieu in the UK. The plane came down to land at this old military airbase smoothly, from having had a window seat it even felt uncomfortably like we were going to land in the sea. At Murcia airport, a ramshackle building desperately in need of renovation, I took a taxi to the local bus stop. Just after I arrived, an English couple Lucy and Sam arrived, and within a few moments we started talking. The weather was perfect, sunny, hot and dry. We chatted and I got to know them better, Lucy was to be giving presentations at the University there in Murcia. I remember discussing with them about medication issues and they seemed to have some insight into my condition – I believe at this point I had wanted to consider making changes to my medication as I had wanted to reduce the anti psychotic medication I take –"olanzapine", the year before.

When I arrived in Murcia, I was soon greeted by Pablo, the brother of Miri, a Spanish friend who Id worked with as a volunteer at the Sue Ryder Foundation in Cavendish, Suffolk. Id previously been to Murcia and stayed with Miri and her family for a holiday a year after completing my volunteering in Suffolk and after working in France. I had arranged to stay with her parents for the first few days in Spain to enable me to find a flat which I could share - the first few days I was in the comfort of Miri's family which was very welcoming. After the weekend had passed, I went flat hunting with Pablo. From and advert at the Biblioteca Pública, we came across a flat inhabited by two young men. We went to take a look at the flat and I quickly decided that this would be a good place to live – close to Zig zag and the sports ground, I snapped it up. Not long after arriving back at the family home in Los Vientos, I rang Juan, my new housemate to be, to confirm that I would like to pay my deposit. Juan greeted me saying he was pleased, and we made the arrangement that I would move in within the next week. A few minutes after I rang Juan, the phone rang, and Miri's mother passed it to me, it was Juan. *"Andrew, I thought I had better ring you now to tell you that, myself and José Maria are gay – does that bother you?"* "No, I said, it doesn't bother me at all." I felt completely intrigued… I remembered at this point my experience of being accused of being gay on the campsite in France and how I flatly denied any gay tendencies. The fact being that this was the beginning of being in denial. Whilst on the one hand I was interested and intrigued, and arguably I had doubts, I refused to accept that I could be inclined that way. But I couldn't help myself, I had so much curiosity I couldn't say no to such an offer.

On the Sunday evening Pablo took me down to Santa Maria de Gracias with my two suitcases and hand luggage. For the first few days I spent time getting used to my new surroundings, and going shopping with Juan and José Maria. I felt more comfortable with Juan, he was more talkative, friendly and open. José Maria was on the other hand more reserved and would not initiate conversation. I also recall how, on admitting to the pair (who were admittedly not a couple) that I had doubts about my sexuality, José Maria shared this with his friend Roberto, who I had the some contact with – he mocked the fact that, being a trusting yet also vulnerable person, I confided in Juan and José Maria about my feelings. This belittled me even more, so I decided to have words with José Maria.
"Who the hell do you think you are taking the rip out of me??? I thought I could trust you, thank a lot." I said in broken Spanish. *"I'm sorry,"* said José Maria. *"This is what Roberto is like."*

"*I don't care what he's like, or who he thinks he is, he was bang out of order.*" José Maria seemed to cower pathetically as I got more and more cross. In actual fact, apart from being in denial I did have a point – being confused about one's sexuality is no fun, so having the piss taken out of one makes it twice as painful. The next day I went into Murcia City and I met my good friend Paula, I had to open up my bank account and transfer some money. We then went for coffee and cake, which Paula being Paula offered to pick up the bill for. Not long after leaving her, I got a text from Juan saying that they were to have lunch soon and did I want to join them. I happened to be on my way home anyway, so I quickly replied I would be around 10 minutes.

José Maria's friend Guillermo had brought pizza for us all. I wasn't immediately attracted to Guillermo, although I was later to find that he had a certain appeal to me. After we ate the pizza, José Maria and Juan sat down on one couch, and Guillermo and me on the other. As we watched the television I noticed out of the corner of my eye that Guillermo was perching closer and closer towards me. I sensed a feeling of complete excitement – this was going to be my first encounter, my first kiss, my first pleasurable experience, from having felt trapped and unable to express how I truly felt. After experiencing how tactile Guillermo was, we went back to my room where we enjoyed each other's company.

After Guillermo had left, José Maria and Juan said that Guillermo had been disrespectful towards me, as he had wanted to take advantage. Being again quite vulnerable yet very intrigued I agreed, as it seemed at this point that both José Maria and Juan were casting doubts as to whether they personally thought I was gay or not. However Guillermo kept coming back to the flat. The next time he came, I was watching television. I'd arranged to see Sam and Lucy who were on their last night in Murcia. Guillermo approached me, stroking me, and said *"Andrew, would you like to go for a coffee later with me?"* I didn't know how to take him, or the idea of more sexual pleasure. I felt scared, afraid- What had I become?! However, I could no resist "temptation". I arranged to meet Antonio that evening, at his apartment at around 10pm I decided I was going to have to make up an excuse with regards to my evening out with Sam, Lucy and also my friend Marisa. I arrived at the bar we had arranged to meet, lying through my teeth I said that I had promised I would be back at the flat to let my flat mate in as he said he had lost his keys. Upon leaving Sam, Lucy and Marisa I went hurriedly to Guillermo's flat, which was a good 25 minutes walk from Murcia city centre. We had a good chat and started to get to know each other better, and now I knew it had become something which I did not know best how to deal with. After a short while, I left Guillermo's apartment in a hurry in spite of him encouraging me to stay. I was scared- I didn't know what had become of me, just that for some reason it was upsetting me a lot and I felt guilty -I needed to escape.

The next day I met my Erasmus friend Cristina who taught me English in my second year at university along with two other girls, Paloma and Esther. Cristina was now studying her masters in Business back at the University of Murcia. When we met- I'd asked her to meet me as I needed to talk to someone, I told her being very economical with the truth about what had happened, saying just that my flat mates had made me feel uncomfortable and that I felt because one of them had made a pass on me I felt uneasy. Cristina advised me that I should look for somewhere else to live. You see, throughout this denial period I lost my confidence, my ability to make decisions, think for myself.....I needed a lot of reassurance. That evening I went to Burger King a little later on with Cristina, and is was there that I met by a very fine chance my old friend from the Sue Ryder Foundation, and her boyfriend Pedro. I was stood

in front of her in the queue when I heard *"Excuse me but would you happen to be Andrew Spriggs?"*
I turned round to my amazement, yes it was actually Elena! We had a lot of catching up to do, that was for sure. I excused myself from Cristina and her friends and we went upstairs where we sat and tried to recover some of the lost ground since 1997. Elena had lost both her parents in the few years preceding me coming to Spain and was now living in Las Torres de Cotillas (in English known as the "Gossiping Towers"). I explained my situation to Elena that I was looking for a new flat and I needed out of where I was. I explained that I felt uncomfortable where I was currently living, and that I felt I could no longer bear to stay there. Elena and Pedro came with me to the flat where I packed my things. Juan tried to stop me from leaving, saying that I was making a big mistake, running away was not the answer. I tried my best to ignore him, saying there was nothing left to say and that I could no longer stay there.

Elena explained when we left the flat that as I hadn't paid any rent, they had given José Maria and Juan the name of someone they knew who was looking for a flat to rent in Murcia. I realised in fact that I had had a lucky escape financially as I still hadn't even paid my deposit. Elena took me to Marisa's flat – Elena did initially assume that Marisa was Spanish, as she blurted out what had happened to me over the phone, Marisa trying very hard to acknowledge and show understanding of what Elena was saying to her! Elena being Elena took control and was forthright - she had definitely proved herself to be a loyal friend.

On arrival at Marisa's flat, in the not so nice barrio of Vista Bella, I became better acquainted to Marisa. Although Marisa's mother is Spanish, home for Marisa was Lytham St Anne's near Blackpool. She handed me a glass of water, and laughed. *"Sorry it's not exactly the Ritz here,"* she said. *"Well beggars cannot be choosers"*, I replied. And so I unpacked what I needed and went so sleep.

The next day was sunny, hot and we went to get food – Marisa was aware that I had to spend time looking for a flat, so after we had had breakfast – this being at 12 noon, we went looking for flats, all over Murcia, in Vista Bella, La Fama, Barrio del Carmen…until we came across two Italians, Luigi and Paolo. The Italians had a dog and we happened to meet them while looking at handwritten adverts that were common in Spain with a phone number that could be torn off at the bottom of the page. We quickly became acquainted and with them, their dog and Marisa we went to the flat that the Italians said they had found. The flat was just across from La Merced – the language and law department of the university. It was a top floor flat, with great views of the city. The landlord greeted us and showed us round, saying how he would bring in furniture in and provide a television. I couldn't believe my luck! We had found our perfect flat, in one day! That night we had a very small party, the Italians provided food and Marisa came round. We stayed up celebrating finding such an amazing flat until the early hours of the morning.

The next day I ate breakfast with Luigi and Paulo and went off to La Merced where I had to sort out my timetable. I had barely been there 30 minutes when I received what appeared to be a frantic message from the landlord, saying "*Come now to the flat*".So I went in a hurry, wondering what all the fuss was about. When I arrived, the landlord, looking (or appearing to look) distraught, announced that he was unable to let us stay there anymore. I was full of disbelief – "How could this be possible?" I said to him. "It's my parents," he stammered. "They don't want to let the house to students. You will have to pack your bags and leave."

I couldn't believe it! Having to leave one flat was bad enough, but a second was just really bad luck. Finally Luigi and Paulo arrived and some frantic phone calls were made, to a friend of the Italians – Luigi and Paulo's friend and also to Elena – both these women were trying desperately to assist. *"You will have to spend as much time as possible looking, Andrew"*, Elena said. Full of advice and positivity as usual, I leant on her for moral support. After we scrambled our clothes and suitcases together, we got in Luigi's estate car along with Paulo and his dog. We spent the next three days looking together… going via estate agencies looking round flats, wandering between neighbourhood to neighbourhood…but it was all fruitless. That evening Elena came to meet me in Murcia, and offered me a bed for the night at hers and Julian's house in the country. *"the appearance of the Italians is not too good, Andrew- that's why I didn't want them to stay with you."* On the third day of looking Marisa came to meet us, and she offered some advice. *"Andrew, its obviously not working trailing round Murcia with Luigi and Paolo and their dog…Do you really want to be spending another night at Elena's?"* A few days prior to meeting the Italians, I had seen an advertisement on a lamppost for a flat in Floridablanca, with two Spanish girls – Laura and Trinni. After I decided to sadly part with the Italians, I went back to the lamppost and called the mobile number listed and spoke with Laura. First impressions did not see too bad, although I had problems understanding Laura with her thick Carthaginian accent. After about three attempts to ascertain where the flat actually was, myself and Marisa arrived, ringing the door bell and going up the musty flight of stairs – the *"hollow bit"* as Marisa and myself joked about – where everyone hang their washing seemed to be full of the smells of cooking and chip fat. This move to live with Laura and Trinni had been done rather in haste in order to solve what had been a mini crisis – I didn't feel at all as though I had had on this occasion, time

The Two Shadows of Success

and opportunity to look around. I couldn't have made a bigger mistake!

My time here in Floridablanca proved to be very unhappy. Whilst I found it difficult to get on and make conversation with Laura – Trinni on the other hand did, although this effort was usually only orchestrated when Laura was not at home. I began to spend less and less time with them and more and more time either out of the flat itself or in my room. Before long – I think it was about a week to two weeks after moving there, I suddenly began to feel very odd. In fact it was one morning I woke up late and felt as though I could not muster up enough energy to go to class. I felt somewhat different to before – just that I couldn't face the day and didn't feel that I could face my responsibilities. I'd arranged to work in a school Las Planchas, listening to kids read. I had already started this off on a bad note, ringing in sick because I couldn't cope with dealing with the challenges of the day and managing this new yet totally unwelcome sinking feeling that seemed to be dragging me down. At this time I'd still been going back to see Guillermo for company, then running off when it suited me. The influence that he had had on me was causing me a lot of doubt in my mind. I couldn't work out all the crazy thoughts I was having – scared, petrified – that I had done something wrong, that people wouldn't accept me for all of this, unhappy and unable to cope with everyday life. If only people had known what was going off. Shortly afterwards I had a test for HIV, arranged by a Spanish GP who seemed to be incredulous at my request, asking me if I'd used protection – well we hadn't but hadn't gone that far but that didn't stop the worrying I had go spiralling out of control –"What if they made a mistake with the test, what if they didn't leave enough time for incubation purposes…" The situation was really becoming quite stressful and at this point I turned to my good friend Marisa who spent a lot of time listening over drinks – and trying to understand lots about how

I was feeling. Marisa could not have known what was going on inside of me, but she nevertheless empathised. On top of all that and feeling continuously like death warmed up, I had financial problems. My lack of forward planning about coming to Spain had been to my detriment in that I was continuously short of money, having had the misguided preconception of the strength of the £ against the Euro and how things were in my eyes cheaper in Spain. Going from day to day felt like climbing Mount Everest, every usual easy challenge felt like a major hurdle to overcome – going shopping, getting up to go to Las Planchas, going to class – well very often I just could not face going.

The situation with Laura and Trinni got to breaking point so I decided that I would have to look for somewhere else to live – I felt like the atmosphere in the house cut be cut by scissors, so I told the girls then that I had been looking for a new flat, with the help of Esther – Esther had helped me in my second year when I needed English tuition at university at home, along with Cristina and Paloma. I also had to coordinate arranging for someone to take my place in the flat – which proved very difficult as Laura and Trinni were always unavailable when I tried to contact them, so I ended up losing my deposit. Esther helped me further –not only with liaising with the landlord about Laura and Trinni's ignorance relating to being present for future tenants to meet them, but then she assisted me in meeting my new flat mates – Antonio, Fernando and Joaquin, who I came to get along with much better. Antonio was a student studying law – a very helpful and confident man, full of good ideas as to how to approach things, and also very supportive – when I later came to admit that I felt suicidal. Fernando again was very friendly, a bit more laid back in his approach but very supportive and we still maintain a good friendship to this day. Joaquin was somewhat quiet and conversation was limited with him, although he was easy to get on with. When

I moved Calle Cronista Rodriguez and met Antonio and his then girlfriend Nadia, I did feel like a whole weight had been taken off my shoulders. At last, in November 3 months after arriving in Spain, I was finally starting to feel settled. However the depressive feelings – wanting to sleep in and not get up, did not disappear. Going back home at Christmas seemed to bring some normality back to my life – I was back home living with mum and dad and I felt more at ease. However this was offset by the feeling that things were changing at home whilst I was away – I went to a family friend's funeral and it made me feel so helpless that I didn't feel able to be seeing how things were changing – my life instead was this confused mishmash in a foreign city, with comparatively little support.

I flew home on 3rd January, about a week before university classes started again. Antonio and Nadia picked me up from the airport, and again I painted a happy picture. That night I made a frantic phone call home, crying incessantly about how unhappy I felt. I had arrived back to a dark cold flat with no-one present, having come from home where I had been staying with mum and dad, seeing friends – the depression hadn't gone though during this time in the UK it had eased as I had brought myself back into 'normal' existence, not the messy confusing state that I had been in Spain.

The next day I decided enough was enough and I presented myself at the Morales Meseguer hospital in Murcia, where I was assessed by a triage GP and then referred to an on call psychiatrist. I will never forget this meeting – the psychiatrist and trainee with her – were so empathetic and patient. As the psychiatrist listened and wrote down what I was telling her – my history as a Bipolar sufferer and being a student in Spain – how I felt the reason for being depressed was due to the change of environment when I went home at Christmas – without mentioning the issues surrounding my sexual identity

– I started to cry. "*Whats up, Andrew?*" She asked. In rather wobbly Spanish I replied that I didn't know, which the frightening thing was I didn't know, I just didn't feel myself. She was as previously stated extremely nice- complimenting my Spanish and then went onto say that she thought I would need support, so she would refer me to a regular psychiatrist at the hospital and to take Seoxat-Paroxetine, an anti-depressant, on a daily basis.

Antonio and Fernando were extremely supportive throughout this period and when I admitted to Antonio that I had suicidal thoughts he really tried hard to help. On one occasion he took me to see my old friend Miri's sister, Sonia a doctor who I talked to briefly about my depression. I met with her at her parent's flat in Molina de Segura. "*Do you know why you are feeling so bad,*" she asked. "*I have absolutely no idea,*" I said – (I was in fact lying to her and to myself). "*I think it's because you went home to the UK and you found that things had changed,*" she said. "*You've come back here to realise you have no control over them, and Andrew life is like that. You're life is at the moment over here, in Spain.*" At that moment Miri's mother came in and the conversation came to an end. I had agreed with her sister about what her reasoning was for my depression, but this agreement was in fact done because at this point I simply had no idea where to start with this depression –or at least partly no idea what had caused what and why I had become consumed by it.

A few weeks later I went back to Morales Meseguer hospital and saw a lovely psychiatrist, Dr Meseguer – who spoke good English, grinning on one occasion that "*My English is not so bad, is it?!*" He gave regular support every month and listened to me, telling me how important it was given how low I felt that I took the anti depressant Seroxat-Paroxetine every single day – I did forget a couple of times and this did in fact set me back by two days each time. Unfortunately to my knowledge at this point in 2004 there were no CPN's – community psychiatric nurses in Spain as in the UK so I was without support in between appointments. As part of the culture in Spain it is expected that the family offer day to day support to the patient concerned but in my case this was not available- which the psychiatrist took into account.

At around this time I had been meeting with Miri's friend, Natalia Asnal – Natalia had signposted me to a psychologist, Nuria Fernandez. Looking back I could have handled things completely differently – as I felt so shamefully low about what had happened, I concealed the truth to Nuria and told her that the issue with Guillermo had all been his doing- that he had tried to convert me to being gay and sexually influence me. Nuria initially asked me when I went out onto the streets did I look at men or women, did I like men or women – again I lied to her and denied any homosexual ideation. So in fact a 32 euro per hour appointment did not actually achieve anything – I hadn't achieved anything except reinforce the self destruct belief that I was in emotional turmoil.

The depression continued on for several months and cumulated when my job at the school ended due to my ill health – who could blame them for that really – on the surface I appeared to be extremely unreliable which is not desirable for any employer. I had also been accused of not ringing in sick on some occasions…this did make me feel like a failure, but I had to remember that this was their view of me, and did not take into account at all the issues which I had been battling with. From my point of view it was unfortunate, although it did reinforce to me the need to remember that employers do not like unreliability. I only wish I could have been more honest with the head teacher – but I had been so unsure of myself I just hadn't known where to start or what would seem suitable to say. The depression however had made me succumb to pour out my problems some people, thus making me very vulnerable – that feeling that you place trust in anyone and everyone as without this you just simply can't cope with the emotional distress and low feelings you have. My flat mate at the time Antonio as previously stated used to help me a lot, He listened to me to how I was feeling and tried to offer advice. I also leant on Cristina and Paloma, I remember telling these lovely girls on one evening how I couldn't bear to face my responsibilities and I could only shut myself in the apartment at Calle Rodriguez Chronista and sleep, afraid to face the next day. *"You have to come out and mix with people, Andrew,"* Cristina said, *"not stay in doors alone."*

One crazy day in spite of my mental ill health I arranged with two casual friends (who knew of Paula -Paula is now my good friend who lives in Staffordshire, married and with two lovely boys), to go skiing in the Sierra Nevada. Skiing??!!! I could hardly cope going to Mercadona and buy groceries, let alone hire a car, and manage that. The churning anxious feeling I had all day long was screaming out to me *"No, Andrew don't do it, you won't cope, I won't let you cope!!!"* I had already hired a car previous and taken Sally and Stacey to Mojácar by the coast, again I was challenging my self to do difficult things whilst feeling so anxious and uncomfortable. I'd hired a Daewoo Matiz, not exactly a speed mobile but it had got us there and back intact, and then I drove us up to the Baloneraios at Archena. Anyway, the trip to Sierra Nevada started when I sat in a cyber cafe in Vista Alegre and we put a deposit down for it. I remember the day I was due to go – I was absolutely dreading the journey. I rang Natalia Gutierrez who was at home at the time. Natalia met me near the Biblioteca Pública and tried to calm me down. *"I'm sorry,"* Natalia. I mumbled. *"I'm just so scared about going."* *"It will be fine,"* she said. *"There are a lot of cars going up there. You won't be on your own anyway will you?" "Andrew, try to get yourself into a routine. Get yourself up at 9am or 9.30am, have some breakfast."* That was precisely it though. I could get myself into a routine! It was hard enough getting up at midday, let a lone 9am or 9.30am. I walked back down Calle Juan Carlos with Marian and she bid me farewell. Sally had rung me the night before and confirmed arrangements, I was to catch the train to Lorca and meet her and Stacey there at the train station there in Lorca. After getting on the Alicante train and just avoiding completely messing up the arrangements, I ran off and found the Lorca train. I was absolutely petrified my pants- on arrival in Lorca I was to drive all the way to Sierra Nevada.

When I got to Lorca, Sally greeted me and we walked to the Ford KA. Stacey was sat in the car, exhausted – the girls had driven up from Malaga. "Andrew, we have a problem, "Stacey said. "You're not insured to drive the car." "What do you mean?" I couldn't believe it. "When we picked the car up from Murcia airport, we weren't aware that you too had to be present in order to be signed up as legally insured to drive the car." I couldn't believe it! What were we going to do?

"Ok, I said, I'll ring them." At first the response was that there was nothing that could be done, but I then asked if they would accept a fax with a signed statement from myself. This was acceptable, to the car hire so I then had to run around Lorca like a mad man, trying to find a shop with a fax. Bearing in mind that it was now 8pm and the shops were about to close. After a frantic search I found a "Papeleria" on the corner of a street close to the station. The shop owner reluctantly agreed to let me use the fax as it was almost time for the shop to close and I also at the same time spoke to the hire car company on the phone trying to ascertain what details were required and managing to scramble a pen and paper together. I must have had to leave the "Papeleria" several times, the shop owner beginning to become impatient. Finally the fax got sent and we got the all clear with about a minute to go before I was about to be kicked out of the shop that I was legally insured to drive the car. It just goes to show what anyone can do even when incredibly low when they set their mind to it.

I was petrified about getting back to the car and having to drive some 300 kilometres in the dark to the mountains near Granada. No, petrified was not the word- I was seriously panicking inside. But the girls were relying on me.

After a shaky start we got going and were fine – at least the fact that the anxiety – either from the car driving or the depression itself had eased a little. The rest of the journey was quite steady – I guess I was doubting my self which I think unnerved the girls, but proud of myself for getting the car and doing it in spite of the raised level of stress. No doubt on arrival when I got to the mountains we found the apartment and I went straight to sleep – much to the annoyance of Sally- they had to drive back down the mountain and pick up Kirsty and Khylie who were experienced skiers.

Although the trip was stressful from start to finish it was an achievement– on the Saturday I was told that the ski pass was not included There were problems that resulted in a dispute over what we were covered re car insurance and number of passengers -I guess she had a point though as it would have been very inconvenient for them to find their way down to the bus station in Granada. In any case we had missed the last bus back to Murcia for them to catch so it would have meant an overnight stay for them. Reluctantly I agreed that they should come with us, being the only one now who felt they should make their own way home. The truth be told I was relieved to be on the way home, the anxiety still churning away inside of me.

It was hard driving back in the dark and there were no street lights on the motorway – a road unfamiliar to myself.

Half way back to Murcia on the Autovia del mediteranneo I swapped driving and allowed Stacey to take over, accepting gratefully a cigarette from Khylie. The relief on getting back Murcia was immense. The anxiety had lifted a little but I still felt low. But I'd done it even though feeling so completely unwell!

The next few weeks I continued to drift – managing a class at the university when I could although I could not manage the early morning starts. I think I made a handful of the 10am lectures and even getting to the school was a real chore for my part time job. If only I'd told them at the school how I'd been feeling – maybe it wouldn't have made any difference, I mean they needed someone there and not off sick all the time. But I had no idea how to explain what was going on inside me and felt so embarrassed. Antonio tried his best to get me out in the evenings, although often he was not there as he was staying at his girlfriend's Nadia's house, or at his family home in Cartagena. They were both nice to me – I guess they too could not be expected to know how absolutely shit I felt, day in day out. From the day when I said to Antonio I wanted to end it, they had been there for me. Antonio was a really dependable person – someone who could be relied upon for advice, a supportive friend – an *"amigo"*.

At Easter in 2004, shortly after the Atocha bombings, I arranged to travel to Italy to visit my Italian friends Gabriela, Daniela, Alessandro and Cristoforo, and then onto Paris to visit Jeremy. It was a welcome break and it did make me feel better, being in the company of good friends. I was glad to be able to have some time away from Murcia. Time away from the four walls of our flat. Time away from the Erasmus scene which I felt so isolated from. Whilst in Italy my depression lifted and I enjoyed parties, coffee shops and eating out. The company was extremely warm, and I felt wanted and loved. Italy seemed to be a more open, warm and welcoming place than Spain. I wished then that I had done my Erasmus year in Italy, but then again what was I basing this decision on? Would I have felt any better if Id spent 6 months depressed in Italy, to come to Spain for a week as a holiday? Would I not have hated being in Italy then? The company helped to lift my mood and I was so well looked after by these sound individuals.

However I came to Spain to face further low mood. Dr Meseguer and Miri's sister Sonia were my main sources of support – although Paula and Marisa came to be very close friends too. As previously stated I saw Dr Meseguer once a month, from January until May. He was very kind and supportive, I used to wait in desperation for the appointments. I used to tell him how much I struggled in the mornings but how I felt a bit better once I'd got up – he used to say how important it was to keep taking the anti-depressant, and he encouraged me to keep active, as did my friend Trish who I accompanied on one occasion to a local gym in Vista Alegre.

There was a further blow whilst in Spain which to this day has been a skeleton in my closet, my school job ended due to my ill health which affected my attendance there – actually I had panicked as my tutor at university had told me my attendance at university was so poor, so I decided that I had to attend classes and stop going to the school – when in fact had I come clean about needing the money, I could have avoided the attendance issue at university. What a mess –two of these modules I hadn't hardly attended- well I learnt from that it is important to be honest with all parties to avoid inconveniencing yourself. If I'd explained that I needed to work because of financial problems then this would not have been an issue. The threat with the university attendance was that the Erasmus grant that I had been awarded could have had to be repaid – and that was £1500, so I didn't want that. I remember at the time panicking about it with a friend but we did end up resolving the issue and joking about it at the same time!

Following working at Las Planchas, things did seem to get better, - the weather improved and classes ended at La Merced. I was sad that the school job had come to an end but I was in a mess with my life so I guess it's a steep learning curve. I have learnt from it and how being open and honest can help others around you to support you. I learnt that I had various negative issues surrounding me which can be resolved – the financial aspect could have been dealt with by asking permission from my tutors to get a job to support me financially and also to give me a structure. And most importantly I would like to say that as strong and stern advice, it is vital for your health to accept who you are and celebrate this. My suffering was extended because I repeatedly refused to accept this and was scared of how others may see this. But had I explained this to my friends, course tutor, head teacher and Psychologist I may have been in a better situation than I was. I wasn't in touch with my emotions, unable to see how I could find solutions living day to day in depressive chaos. I also had no proper structure in my life. So I would say it is highly important to look at yourself and what does and doesn't suit you and make comparisons between situations. Do you like routine? Do you prefer to be busy doing things or do you not mind about having no structure in your life? Do you like adventure or do you prefer stability? Do you like the challenge of living in other countries or do you prefer to be more in control in the familiarity of your own environment? Do you like to know where things are and what time they are open from and until? How would you feel about being unwell? Would it be a good idea to plan for this eventuality? The key and overall outstanding lesson I learnt was preparation. I learnt that in future I should look at planning activities at times when abroad to avoid losing the daily structure. I use internet banking now to keep an eye on my bank account. In future too I would disclose to those who should know about what I'm going through so they can best help and support me and look at structuring my day in advance to avoid going through further bouts of depression.

I had however managed to spend at least some time travelling across Spain to see friends in Cadiz, Salamanca and Madrid. These were friends from my 2nd year at university who were Erasmus students there- Javier, Yolanda, Isabel and Mari Carmen and an American chap called James whose flat I stayed in when visiting them in Salamanca. I also went to Barcelona and Cartagena with Marisa and I have to say the joy of seeing friends there and seeing new things helped me to feel better.

In the few weeks prior to my departure from Murcia, things really picked up with my emotional health. The weather improved, and I got see more of my friends Paloma, Cristina, and Frederico. Frederico often invited me to play tennis and then eat in his flat – I thoroughly enjoyed his friendship, as well as Cristina and Paloma's. Frederico and Paloma were and are a couple (although myself and Cristina lost contact with the pair). Myself, Frederico and Paloma went out for dinner (a few nights before my departure) drinking and then with Cristina – these last few weeks were some of the most awe inspiring times. My secret identity crisis was coming one step closer to being out in the open. The daily mish mash feeling was disintegrating and my spirits were on the up.

The day before my departure I came back to the flat to find my other flat mate to be in a state. He had been in a fragile way for a long time and had told me that he had been seeking help for this. In fact my departure could not have come at a worse time – on this day he really needed support and he begged me not to go. Unsure of the reason why he wanted me to stay so desperately, I went with him to the beach and we sat, smoked like chimneys, and talked. I think looking back Fernando was in turmoil- he had been in a relationship with a local Murciano girl, Lolita, who had been at the flat quite a few times, but this may have been part of the problem however it could not proven to be the case. On the day of my departure Fernando's friend took me with him to the bus station. I said my good byes to Jorge – I think I must have said about 10 sentences to him the whole time I was in the flat. Antonio had left a letter saying good bye, he had to be elsewhere which was not unusual for him as he was an quite industrious chap. I was in fact moving temporarily to France - to do complete a French course which I was obliged to do as part of my degree course. This course was quite well structured and I ended up meeting up with some others from my degree course – a pleasant time in all where I got to meet students from across Europe. It was quite a fun time visiting places and taking part in theatre productions and attending French classes. While in France it came to me that I felt the time was approaching that I could feel ready to come out about my sexuality. I had actually disclosed to Paula and Marisa in Murcia about what had happened earlier in the year with Guillermo- both had been extremely supportive and had said that it was not something that could be ignored. In Spain Paula had lived literally a stone's throw from me in Vista Alegre and I used to visit her on a regular basis and we used to have regular catch ups. She like Marisa was very supportive of my health condition and my disclosure.

Following the French course in Nancy, I returned home and decided that the time was right now to come out. I had feared for so long how people may react, that they may not want to understand or may turn their backs on me. How wrong was I! My school friends were the first to know- David and Steve, then my university friends, Paula, Marisa, Kim, Jeremy and Ceris and my old friends in Spain. I will never forget my friends saying what a life changing thing it is to become gay.

When I arrived back home after being in France, I had an urge to speak to Guillermo. The poor guy, how I'd messed him around, dithering as to what was right for me. I don't think he ever realised what an integral part he played in changing my life forever. I had an urge to be with him, to speak with him, be with him and most of all make love to him. I still had Juan's number on my old nokia phone, so I rang him upon my arrival into Gatwick airport from Strasbourg. He was naturally suspicious but did give it to me. I later heard from Guillermo that Juan had rung him telling him that he had disclosed his number to me.

Getting back into studying at university was a relief- certainly having the familiar surroundings helped a lot. The first term of my final year at university seemed to race by, whilst settling back into university life and enjoying living in the local student neighbourhood I had met some Spaniards who were on their Erasmus year. I went with Marisa to see them regularly and we often ate in their home and spent time practising Spanish. I shared a house with Marisa and Jeremy- neither had previously known each other, I was their connection, Marisa from Murcia and Jeremy was a friend from 1st and 2nd year. It was great as we all got on well, at least to start with anyway. Jeremy was cool about me having come out as being gay and there was a lot of in house banter. We enjoyed drinking in the local pubs. As a friendship group we all became strong and stuck together. I was also back under Dr Belfringham's care. She was ready again to see me on a weekly basis and there as a support- to this day she has been the most supportive GP I have ever had. Aside from the usual fallouts as housemates over stupid stuff where we spoke didn't a few weeks things were generally ok, particularly so after I had a melt down as

The Two Shadows of Success

a result of university stressors. This had been as result of two complaints I made about two lecturers at University one for two separate departments. The lecturer was very well known and very experienced and it was quite a challenge to question her, yet it did make me all the more determined to prove her wrong. I did get a satisfactory conclusion – my future exam work was to be marked by an external examiner and the complaint was listened to and accepted. Gradually however during the second term I started to lose sleep, some nights maybe just getting an hour, when the second concern presented itself. The second issue was with a Spanish Literature lecturer, who was teaching in the university as part of an exchange with university in Latin America. I'd put a tremendous amount of effort into the presentation I'd done with the then Natasha Oddison, only to find he had given me a 3rd plus also marking me down on language not content in my assignment. It was after all my final year and, amongst all of us undergraduates the tensions and people's emotions were running very high. Everyone knew how much the final year counted towards the degree. I remember clearly the Friday in March when I'd had yet another sleepless night and had gone to the university leisure centre for a swim. I made it to the Spanish language class run by Jorge Espinosa and found a seat fortunately next to my good friend Paula. Paula knew straight away that I wasn't right. I was in fact on the verge of breaking down, and true those words straightaway after the end of the class she took me into Jorge's room. *"Andrew, its ok to have had enough you know, there's no shame in it."* *"Have you got an appointment to see anyone,"* She asked.

"I've got a doctor's appointment at 10.45," I blurted out.
"Right, well Rosie will stay with you till I can come out of Galician and Ill come up with you to see your GP" she said. I went downstairs to the bottom of the languages building, very tearful and feeling very sorry for myself. *"Andrew, you've done so well,"* Rosie reassured me. She stayed with me and

accompanied me to the student lounge where we bumped into Ceris and Mary who offered their much needed support. Paula came from her class at 10.30 and I went with her the doctor's surgery where Dr Belfringham offered her support and advised I would need a medication increase. That weekend I spent at Paula's, Marisa also came as did Rosie and Giles and we had a Spanish tapas evening. I was and am so lucky to have such supportive friends and can describe Paula and Marisa as two amazing young ladies, and by the end of the weekend I was feeling much better and more stable.

Fortunately things calmed down after this weekend, in spite of a fruitless meeting with the head of department where I questioned the way I had been assessed– there had been a number of other complaints from other students about presentations not being recorded, amongst other concerns... I did not feel that following this I had received a satisfactory answer given the sheer hard work, effort and stress involved in completing the two pieces of work. Unfortunately for me this did not get resolved to my satisfaction and I was left feeling unnecessarily bitter.

The last few weeks of term passed more smoothly, I had been in touch with Charles Cunningham the welfare tutor, along with Nigel Huntley who had arranged for my remaining assignments to be done in side rooms. The day of my last exam – French Cinema was a bit of an anti climax, I had gone into the university village with two friends and a few others and we'd had lunch… it was all finally over… 4 years of hard graft coming to an end.

I learnt here that putting in formal complaints is extremely stressful, that is not to say that they were not justified, just that it is important to see what outcome you hope to achieve. I was not the only person to complain about one of the complaints and emotions and stress levels were running extremely high amongst all of us in the fourth year. The fourth year was after all counting for 75% of our overall grade. It did however make me poorly and so with this in mind it is important to ask – what are you complaining about? What will this achieve? Would it be better to prioritise complaining and look after what is having most impact on your so as to avoid perhaps some of the stress?

In the weeks and months following graduating I felt the blues and nostalgia about university life. I'd had a structure, security and many friends as a result of my studies and that all appeared to be coming to an end. I attended graduation after a talk with my mum – I'd felt very bitter following the controversy of the final year at having been awarded a 2:2, in spite of practically everyone telling me how well I'd done against all odds suffering from Bipolar and getting through university. She was quite frustrated that I could not see how much progress I'd made. The truth was I was wrapped up in the disappointment of final year grade obsession which was preventing me from seeing what a massive, major achievement I had seen through. But I do look back and try to see what I went through – the sleepless nights, physical ill health and depression which, given my year in Spain too, was just the icing on the cake. Moreover, having faced the major hurdle of returning to university after having been sectioned is something quite victorious in itself. My mother reminded me to look back at all my efforts and be proud of my success at university – even if I thought it was marred a bit here and there.

During the summer of 2005 I went travelling around Italy and organised flights from Venice to Barcelona and then from Barcelona to Alicante in order to attend a Spanish wedding in Murcia, visiting friends and generally enjoying the free time following my degree. I met up with Gabriela and Daniela in Italy – this time I'd been unable to see Alessandro and Cristoforo as they were both working away from their home town of Padua.

When I returned to Italy from Spain I arranged with the help of Daniela a trip round Italy to Rome, Pisa, Florence and Lake Garda.

Upon my return to the UK I was tasked with starting planning for my PGCE- I had previously been given the opportunity to teach in Canada or start my PGCE. I chose the latter as I'd had doubts about where I would be posted in Canada – I had gone to London to have an interview and been successful but felt it was time to start thinking long term regarding my future I'd spent some time getting prepared but I went on to suffer a set back with a summer job collapsing and being shouted at by an irate pub owner. Unfortunately this knocked my confidence and left me in a fragile state once again requiring support from mental health services. I was then faced with the scrutiny from the head of the PGCE course as to my suitability for the course and so this presented indeed a great challenge on me to get myself better.

I went onto start my PGCE, late starting, determined to prove the head of department wrong. I had a lot of catching up to do when I got there. My accommodation was at the College not too far from the city centre. The environment to me seemed like the ideal place to be studying- it had lots of character- and it was not only the picturesque sights that were appealing but the student life was buzzing. As a PGCE student however although in some ways having the luxury of having a day off in the week, my late arrival had not done me any favours – I was thrown into assignments, seminars, lectures and teaching practice. The pace of the course was fast and it was very important to be on top form at all times. My first school placement was to be at a school fairly local to college. Id arranged to cycle (I'd brought my bike down to campus) to the Education College where I'd meet Simone, Oliver, Stuart and Sean. I remember that first trip to school, where I chatted with the others and got to know them. The truth was that my confidence was at zero due to having been grilled by the course leader as to my suitability for the course and also because of the incident at the pub over the summer. To start with at the secondary school I was observing lessons in the Languages Department, to be honest I felt a mixture of feeling petrified of the students and exhausted at the early starts. My tutor also seemed quite unenthusiastic and demotivated although I felt he was approachable. After I had observed one of all the teacher's lessons, it was time for me to take my lesson. Upon arrival at the classroom I found my tutor to be absent which panicked me. After a few minutes a classroom support worker arrived and the lesson began. Whilst trying to motivate 30 students to my horror two students were smearing tipex across the desk, and throwing sticks. Another student was drawing pictures of penis on his exercise book. Welcome to secondary school teaching I thought! At the end of the lesson the classroom support worker gave me some feedback, she said that my teaching had been good-Id held it together, but I was not feeling very good inside – like a volcano wanting to continuously erupt. I did not believe enough in myself to see the course through.

Looking back if I'd felt stronger and more resilient I would have stuck at it, but my last week at the Educational College saw me falter and crumple under the pressure of the course and classes. After an emotional weekend with friends where I looked at the situation I was in - assignments flying up, presentations to do, lectures to attend and classes to do I felt I could no longer commit to the course and its demands, so I quit.

Upon telling my tutor that I could not continue due to health concerns, which he fully understood and agreed, I went back to Sophie's class and told the group I'd just quit. I went down to the cafeteria, had a coffee and started to brainstorm ideas for what I could do. At the end of the class my fellow course mates came down and sat and chatted to me. "*Do you feel relieved?*" they asked. "*Yes, big time,*" I said.

"*Then you know it was the right decision. Andy, listen it might not have been the right time for you do the PGCE.*" I pondered on what they had said and I knew in my heart of hearts that I'd made the right decision. Teaching is an incredibly stressful profession and one where there is no let up from pressure –teaching, discipline, marking, planning, attending meetings – it all adds up and is for many a lot to handle. By problem solving the issue I got rid of the horrible anxiety I was having to manage and therefore was able to go on and consider other more suitable jobs. I learnt a lot from this experience - it is possible for people with mental health conditions to teach, but it depends a lot on the environment and time in the life of this person and more importantly what support is available for them. You have to be mentally prepared and have the belief that you can see through the demands of the PGCE to start with. However, if this is not suitable career option, recognise that you have learnt something new about yourselves that you did not already know. Yes it was a knock to my self confidence but it helped to shape what I decided to do next. In short it wasn't meant to be.

After a night's good send off with my course mates mum and dad came down and collected me and all my stuff. The relief from quitting soon changed to a feeling of fear and low confidence – I'd suffered a big knock to my self esteem and I was back at home where I had to start from scratch. Certainly being back at home was the best place for me although the only solution anyway.

Chapter 5

RETURN TO WORK

I got back into working quickly after leaving the Educational College although I found it hard – I started back working for a local cast iron company, temping in the office, and working at the local leisure centre café. My nerves started to get the better of me; I was very emotional, shaky, nervous. At the cast iron company my boss Aaron was very understanding and told me to slow down and do one thing at once. I was so anxious to make a good impression, so worried about failure given the set back I'd had earlier in the year. I told him about how I couldn't switch off at night and was worrying myself sick about the smallest of things. Aaron was very kind to me, sensitive and caring. Just before Christmas he bought me a crate of beer, and he had told me how he wanted to help me prepare for working life. He obviously only wanted what was best for me. Fortunately too I had been to my GP and requested a referral to mental health. A few days later, a CPN came to do an assessment, and I was allocated a worker, Chris Morgan, who was (he's now retired) an Approved Mental Health Professional. He is a lovely calm man who was great at listening and understanding my problems and concerns. My job at the cast iron company was only temporary and after Christmas of 2005 I was out of

Andrew Spriggs

work again. Mum and pops encouraged me to get a job – they thought and rightly so that that was the answer. I'd been in the job centre and seen an advert for an administrative job at a local oil depot, initially advertised as Purchase Ledger, then to be changed to a Receivables position. Jayne at Blue Arrow had secured me some temping work after a few weeks and had said that I'd got a temping job at Royal Mail for a further week, however I had an informal interview booked at the oil depot and went in to meet John and Sue. We had a brief chat and they agreed for me to start on the following Monday.

I had a very happy time at the oil depot. As part of a three man team, the office dynamics were good – an equal male and female spread. In my team there was myself and Alex as administrators, and John was the Receivables Team Leader. Alex was the Senior Administrator. The job was steady and I was well supported. Basically my role consisted of banking all the cheques and allocating payments against invoices. In the Purchase ledger team there was Denise who was the team leader and Sue, as previously mentioned. Rosina, sat across from myself and Alex was a trainee accountant, Niko was her line manager, whilst Alfonso (soon after my arrival he changed jobs) was the manager. Isaac Hunter was soon to take over Alfonso's job as the manager. There was constant light hearted banter particularly between myself, Alex, John, Denise, Sue and Rosina, particularly about making drinks and general banter about male / female stuff. It was a great place to work and I felt comfortable and accepted. Chris Morgan supported me greatly by reinforcing the positives, advising about strategies I could use like deep breathing and focusing on my achievements – he said at this point that I was doing well to be in full time work.

However my enjoyed time at the oil depot was due to come to an end when my contract could not be extended due to budget cuts. In spite of being asked to help out in Credit Management and getting on very well with Esmé and Katia who worked in that department, I left the company as they had advised I would have to do. Esmé had asked with my degree in French and Spanish what was I doing working there! Well if she had 3 days spare I could have told her!

So I left the oil depot and went to work for another local company financial company during this period my CPN changed from being Chris (who went on secondment) to Janis. Janis was a great support to, very open and down to earth, and we would often meet at the pub after work. I have to say from day 1. I absolutely hated this job, environment and work colleagues. There was a lot of politics and a lot of disagreements and ill feeling between members of staff, I realised I would be better off elsewhere. It was during this time at this third employment that I embarked on my first proper relationship, with what appeared to be a charming, cute half Brazilian half German guy, Tomas. I'd initially met him on line and driven to Scunthorpe to meet him. It felt exciting meeting someone foreign. Tomas worked in a factory to the north of Scunthorpe in Quality Control. The second time I met him we met in Sheffield and spent a romantic weekend together in what was a crummy b & b in a southern suburb of Sheffield. It was very romantic, erotic and at first seemed right and amazing.

However shortly afterwards my job started to go pear shaped and I buckled under the pressure of my job and the emotional drain of being in a relationship. My Mum and Dad were justifiably concerned and advised I should think twice about pursuing things with Tomas. Tomas had become very possessive, demanding and controlling and sent me so many emails that I could not cope with it at all. Some of them were just questions like *"Why havn't you replied to the previous email yet." "Why havn't you acknowledged me yet? Why this, Why that?"* As it impacted onto my job which I didn't like either, things soon toppled sideways, so needing me to take time off. I soon ended things with Tomas and we were briefly apart. The situation at work became unbearable and I ended up, upon the consent of the Finance Manager, walking out. It hadn't been a helpful environment to be in. The day after I left I met with Janis, she said that she thought it was an appalling job to do – collecting money off people and having to assert myself and put up with all those office shannigans. Making drinks for some but not making drinks for others, remembering that every fourth drink I make I need to include certain others!

Around December 2006 at the time I left my job, I moved into my new home near the local College, which was a property that my parents had very kindly bought to let out to me. The cul-de-sac is a stone's throw from the local College and the Chamber of Commerce. I became friendly with one of my neighbours, Sandy who got to know myself and Tomas. We often went to Sandy's for food or she came to ours. It was in January when Tomas told me that he had inherited several million pounds from the death of his grandparents. I remember when he told me I did find it a little odd that they had left it all to him as he had his parents and two sisters. He confided in me that he didn't know how to go about managing the money, that it was been held by the banks of Nigeria and Brasil. Now this may seem blatantly obvious to many that it seemed a little dodgy to say the very least. But me being me I wanted to believe that it was real and genuine and that the money would make us both very happy and secure. Tomas made plans to buy Sandy's house as he wanted to live close to me and he put my name down on a joint account at the then local Bradford and Bingley bank for the money which was to be sent across. Whilst all this was going on I had started a temporary job at a consultant company in administration, making frequent trips to the Bradford and Bingley branch to speak to the advisors and manager. However the money never arrived at the branch in spite of several so called attempts by Tomas to ascertain where the problem was. He made up a story that the money was being held by a bank in Scunthorpe, that he had had to call the Police to force the bank manager to give Tomas his money so that he could transfer it to Bradford and Bingley branch. Tomas wrote me a blank cheque and had left it in my home, he said that I could put some money back in my account with an amount of several thousand pounds. However I got into a mess with my bank – went over my overdraft limit and my bank wrote to me asking if they could be of any help. Shortly after this I was forced to close my bank account and pay off the outstanding debt, with two members of staff present. It was one of the most humiliating days of my life, soon to be followed by the most humiliating – going into Natwest with Tomas, watching who I thought was an honest caring guy be arrested on Valentine's day. He was under arrest on suspicion of cheque deception. I thought he had gone with me to Natwest to withdraw a small amount of money. He had actually asked for 4 million!! That day was a living nightmare, I was running round like a mad man, I ran into a solicitor's office and blurted out that I needed to speak to someone. But there was nothing anyone could do. In desperation I rang my mum's friend Monica and divulged all that had happened. She in turn rang my mum who came later to the Police station – Tomas had my house key and the Police were suspicious as to why he had this. That evening I went to Sandy's and between us we decided that we had to try and help him. At this point we still believed that he was innocent. Sandy rang the Brazilian Embassy, who I was later to find out rang the Police station to check on Tomas. Tomas had said that the money he had inherited was in a will document that his father had. When I picked him up from the Police station, crying as he was, myself and Sandy tried to reassure him that everything would be ok, all this mess would be cleared up. Only this was the beginning of the end – at work I received some incredibly dodgy emails from the Bank of Nigeria and the Bank of Brasil, and following Tomas' temporary disappearance to Bournemouth to see supposed friends Francisca and Tadeu, Sandy expressed her concern over Tomas's integrity. *"Do you trust Tomas?"* She said to me twice. The first time I had replied that yes I had, the second I said that I had doubts. *"Why don't we get your mum to come round,"* she said. I rang home and mum came round, equally concerned about this apparent fabrication. We discussed everything that had happened, all the discrepancies, weird unusual events – things like Tomas saying that his sister Anna who is an air steward would come to Chesterfield and invite myself, my friends Katy and Dan for meal. Not surprising it was that Anna never appeared, Tomas' excuse was that the plane Anna had been on had had to make an emergency landing in the US. He told me that he had contacts including a man at Toyota and he said that he could get me a job working in HR there at Toyota in Derby. Sandy had contacted Toyota and they said that they did not know of any such person. Another of the emails made reference to an employee at Deutsche Bank. I rang Deutsche Bank and found that this person did not exist. Tomas had also lied about the situation with the Police, that the solicitors had phoned him telling him he didn't need to report back to the Police Station, when actually all along he did and subsequently a wanted file was issued for his arrest.

Mum and Katy both told me that I had to go to the Police and tell them everything. And everything meant everything. I borrowed a pc and printed out every email that I'd ever had with Tomas, courtesy of a friend from a shop where I'd been volunteering. Bearing in mind these emails were very personal and some with sexual innuendo, I was extremely embarrassed at having to give this information to the Police. But that was the price I had to pay to clear my name. When preparing a statement with the Police I broke down desperate not to have the finger of blame pointed at me. The Police man was stern with me and I told him that I swore blind that I was not implicated. I provided evidence including emails that Id received and a so called fake bank document from the Bank of Nigeria. I also had Tomas' work card which said he had worked for Toyota in Brasil.

But as Sandy had said, amidst all the lies he had told and fabrications made, there will have been a strand of truth in what he was saying.

I learnt some very hard lessons here. Internet dating is very risky and lending money to people is too. I put my trust in someone unwittingly and had to face to harsh consequences. Looking back I feel I was maybe pre-empting a relationship when really I should have let it develop naturally. There will always be options to meet new people in life and getting to know someone naturally without all that online pressure is looking back a better way to approach it. Relationships are hard at the best of times and meeting potential partners is hard enough, but more straight forward than a smiling distant picture and a few sweet fa's. Lending money I have since learned should be to those only that you know inside out. Yes I have been burnt here and hope that my lessons will be a testament to others to prevent such occurrences. I also learnt that finances should be kept separate and as such joint accounts should be avoided at all costs.

So, with my name cleared I tried to move on, finding it difficult to control my emotions, I did some temping work for a role with the health service, then within a security office at a centrally located company in my home town. Soon afterwards I landed on my feet with a job at a local company. It was a permanent full time role and I was surprised I got it as I'd got my wires crossed about the interview time, turned up at 3pm instead of 2pm. However it was a confidence booster or at least it seemed like it was. I was working within two sub departments. I was soon to learn that I was the only person in that department with two work loads – two work loads, two new managers to the department, both trying to prove themselves. Looking back I probably wasn't in a strong position mentally. While I was doing more than others I was very impressionable to others. The first meeting I had about my workload did not go well and in my vulnerable state it felt like I was being cornered. Holly one of my managers was quite critical and Julie, the other manager said I needed to seek too much clarification. With the principal manager who was now on my case, I left the room distressed and went out into the yard where I was approached by a worker manager most concerned that I was upset. This got back to this acting director who put her concerns to me in writing, which was all very official. I was emotionally very vulnerable, and as I was soon to find out, this was also not to be the job for me. The counsellor at work, Ellen was about the only person that I felt I could trust. She had previously said that I had a lot of support – she was referring to the level of work that I was being given, however this was not shared by Diana, the principal manager. I had asked for a 50-50 split whereby I would have one change of working direction, however this was not accepted and I was given a mentor who would oversee my work, moreover I would be required to change role every day. I felt that there was a lot of pressure on me given the two roles I had, and so it was not a good position to be in. I had been seeing the company nurse on a regular basis and had placed trust in them.

Following the second meeting where I was supported by the company nurse things temporarily improved, however at this stage my health finally could not stand anymore stress – I went to a colleague's house and got no sleep whatsoever following the previous night where I had stayed at another friend's house.

My work colleague dropped me off near a local shopping centre and I spent some time wandering round aimlessly. I knew I felt unwell if honest and I felt high. The thing was that I had been subjected to – at least in my opinion severe bullying and stress which had reduced my ability to function properly. I'd previously asked to be put in one department and the company nurse said that she would support this. I came back on the train and after an angry confrontation with the ticket officer over a sign which stated that ticket holders could not claim compensation for delayed trains – as I was commuting to work.

When I got home I rang my friend Katy in a euphoric state about ideas I had and how wonderful things were going to be as I was planning to give up smoking, but upon having yet another argument with the bank over a standing order which had not been set up, I lost it. Bipolar Affective Disorder had unravelled itself upon me and I had let it. The drinks at my work colleague's Cathy's house had not helped, coupled with the work related stress were heading me for a serious wobble. I rang Ellen and she offered emotional support which is what I needed, and lots of it, telling her the bank issue was the final straw. I rang Katy and against better judgement drove to their home. She in turn drove me to mum and dad's where I stayed the night. That night I slept well, 10 hours or so and the next day I rang Ellen and told her I was feeling better. However that night I was struggling again, so much, ruminating, I ended up ringing Ellen at 3am. As you can imagine this was not what she'd hoped and she said words to the effect that she didn't know what she could do to help me. I went into work on the train like a gibbering wreck, finding it very hard not to openly cry. A colleague saw me when off the train and gave me a lift up to work. I walked up with her to the offices, found my line manager and told her I'd not slept well and been feeling suicidal. She said straight away for me to see Ellen, or rather the poor Ellen (after having had to deal with me all this time!) who self certified me as sick for a week.

I went on the sick, but what was about to happen seemed to me to be both unbelievable and outrageous. I was called by a colleague of Ellen's and asked to come in for a chat. She said how sorry she was that she had not been there for me the week before. Whilst being lead to believe that she had my best interests at heart, she had been instructed to question me on my medical fitness. The nurse asked to sign papers so she could access my medical records, and at that point asked me to call the Crisis Team so she could speak to them. I rang them, and they refused to speak to her, and told me to tell her that. She then issued me with a form and told me to write down my GP's and Psychiatrist's details. She went on to say that it was questionable whether I was fit to be working. Not surprisingly I was not in a very good place after this and in a distressed state. She asked me if I was at risk of self harm, I said yes, she then rang for an ambulance, the paramedics came to her office and took me to the local hospital.. The Paramedics didn't say anything to me, and then when we arrived they were happy to let me out and go home. I guess they must have thought that was the best thing to do- they could see that being in that building with someone who is supposed to be there to help was not actually helping me. I did end up staying in the hospital for a while where I saw the Crisis team and I told them everything that had happened. They were very supportive I told them that I had been advised to give up my course that I loved, the CPP, and she had gone on to say that I had agreed to the role in the first instance so it was my choice.

I know I chose to have a job, I chose to work hard and also be happy and it was unfortunate that I could not progress further within this company. I also learnt important office skills using Microsoft packages, as well as unique HR work experience. I attended a lot of meetings and whilst there enjoyed the busy role and learnt from a personal view point to avoid ruminating and any alcohol intake when stressed – this just aggravates the situation.

This incident at this company was extremely traumatic and to this day I still often think about what happened there– the memories have faded now but the scar of it all is still there. My worker, Chris Morgan at the time had said to me that I should get away, whilst still being supported by the Crisis team. The Crisis Team were an amazing support and if it had not been for them then I would have been back in hospital, although one of the nurses did suggest a brief spell on a psychiatric ward might be beneficial, I managed to keep away. Chris knew what had gone on at work and he knew, along with the Crisis Team that I had had a difficult time there. But at the end of the day I had to move on – I certainly did not want to be dwelling on it.

Financially things had become really tough, I wasn't claiming any benefits- I didn't even know what I could be entitled to- and my sick pay from this company soon came to an end. I'd still got to pay the remainder of the CPP course I'd been doing as the company had refused to pay the remainder as I'd left by then. Being penniless is no good to anyone but I found the staff at the finance department at university sympathetic and they agreed a very gradual payment plan. I continued with my course throughout the emotional turmoil and in spite of a couple of setbacks where I had vivid flashbacks of the ambulance day I managed to work, although still utterly broke. Following working for this organisation I luckily found a job temping stuffing envelopes, it was full time and was fairly local. I enjoyed going there and found the staff friendly – it was located in a small hamlet called Sutton Scarsdale. My job was to simply send out questionnaires to service users of the health service. The permanent staff had quite a task though, they had to manage the survey helpline and often fielded phone calls from poorly people, some of whom were housebound and very lonely. The job progressed and while doing it I continued with my HR CPP course, managing a payment plan of £10 per week to pay off my course. I had decided in February 2007 that I wanted to pursue a career helping others, in social care. I had applied for 2 jobs – one as an assessment worker and one as a Care assistant for a local care agency. I had wanted to try out this type of work – my mum's good friend Monica had suggested this. Me being me I wanted to progress following the unpleasant state of affairs at the previous company I wanted to try something different. The problem that I was later to find was that I had yet again gone in head first, rushed in not having thought about the job and the demands it would bring – (but then I guess sometimes you don't know until you try?). I had the interview for the job as a assessment worker on the same day as my assessment at a local University for the Recruitment and Selection module, and at the same time as the interview for the Care Agency. The care agency came back to me and said they could offer me employment. When my line manager called the next day and said they wanted to offer me the assessment worker role, I was absolutely over the moon! I then had to make the decision to contact the care agency and tell them I'd been offered another role. As were mum and dad, they were very proud. At this point I had started another temping job working at Text Processing for the local Council, as I had to wait so long for the Occupational Health and CRB checks to come through. However when I worked here at Text Processing I suffered flash backs and got upset very easily. The lady who was supervising me was very nice, albeit a bit stressed – she was covering her colleague who was having an operation. Emotionally I was quite unstable and would get upset over the smallest of things. Her boss was very good and would tell me to take a short break if I felt like this. I disclosed to them that I had had problems in a previous job. One morning I woke up after having felt low the evening before and felt so weepy I didn't feel able to drive, so I contacted Mandy and told her I was not up to driving. I managed to get a GP appointment and saw Dr Williams. She asked if I'd been feeling suicidal, I said yes and she contacted my Social Worker Chris Morgan. Chris had been amazing with me and told me that my thoughts and feelings about how I'd been treated at this company were completely normal, and that they were like ripples in a pond. He congratulated me on the course and said that he would arrange for an appointment with Dr Inderjit, the locum Consultant Psychiatrist. I went to a local hospital for the appointment with Chris and found Dr Inderjit to be a very helpful and caring man. He dicussed my medication and thought stopping / distraction strategies. I went on to work following this appointment and completed the text processing job, and into the assessment worker job. After a long wait I started. The pace of this social work position came on fast and it felt to me from day one a bit threatening. It wasn't like an office job where you are in the safety of an office without being expected to go out and assess other's needs, I had a caseload of service users to see. Initially I was protected from this but after spending a few weeks shadowing others and assisting with jobs for other social workers my caseload was dropped on me. Being in this fight or flight mode, unable to problem solve or believe in overcoming the big massive anvil of a problem that was facing me, I cracked. My boss had become quite unsupportive and made reference to a day off I had taken off sick as me not being able to cope with the pressure. It is a really horrible demoralising feeling that you feel you are not capable of doing a job. *"You can stay Andrew, but no sickness."* She boomed. My colleagues were however very supportive and we had a few long conversations about the situation. There were things that could have been done, and as far as training was concerned apart from some shadowing there was little – I had asked for someone to shadow me, this appeared not to have been possible and was certainly not something my boss was prepared to offer. However I was clearly not ready mentally or emotionally for this job. My confidence was at rock bottom, I had little self esteem and I didn't believe in myself. Maybe I was as much to blame for jumping in head first? It all cumulated in me bursting into tears in the office and feeling rather demoralised. I didn't have the confidence to argue and she strengthened her argument by saying that Id taken a day off sick because I couldn't cope with the pressure. As already stated my colleagues didn't like her very much and were shocked to hear later on that I'd left. Hannah who had started with me as an assessment worker was very supportive and rang me telling me how much everyone was missing me. But I do look back and realise I wasn't ready mentally and had I been more confident this may have carried me along, at least a lot further. After taking a week off sick I relented completely and left this work place, feeling pretty low and dreadful. It felt very humiliating at this point knowing that I had been ousted – This battered person going from job to job, sometimes lasting a few weeks, having low confidence and feeling anxious. The final job that I did before I realised I needed to take some time off work was a customer service role for a local shoe making company where I was in actual fact probably not well enough to be working and really struggled. I had had it mentally and it was Jane from the agency that said that if I didn't take the time to look after myself, I would (as I had done) go from job to job. My parents had always said they wanted what was best for me and we agreed that being off work for a while whilst being financially limiting was the best solution. But the work place is often a challenging place and unless you're envelope stuffing you need to be 100% well. By revisiting the work place and leaving on ill health grounds time and after time, this damages your soul and your self esteem greatly leaving a trail of feeling worthless, feeling like you've failed and are unfit for work. I know that I am fit for work – well I am now, and I have come to realise in the past some people have often made me feel otherwise to protect themselves. I have found from my experience that some reasonable adjustments are not popular with those that do not require them -sometimes they are non existent, sometimes there has been an independent service to support which helps an awful lot but still I feel suitability for a job is crucial. It can be viewed those getting adjustments as receiving special treatment and can only be maintained temporarily, as each organisation can justify things according to the needs of their business. However I learnt from these jobs to take things at a slower pace, be kinder to myself and listen to the professionals. I had been pushing and pushing myself to the extreme limit of my mental capacity. I learnt so much about myself and what jobs would be most suitable. After all, if we never fail, we never learn and then go onto succeed.

It is certainly true that this experience shaped me in many ways. I learnt to avoid taking on too much i.e. doing a full time job and course at the same time whilst making the most of any in work support such as a mentor. I also learnt the importance more importantly to stick with a job but and be honest with yourself at the same time, and say how you feel things could be improved whilst not bending a bicycle that isn't broken- I'd previously been working happily before this incident arose and was happy there. Why did I feel the need to leave? What advantages would the job give me? Am I ready for that job? Would the travelling be more pressure?

During my time off work where I experienced financial challenges as many can empathise, I volunteered at Oxfam and worked 8 hours a week at a pub restaurant near the main motorway. I had a very good manager here who kept my job open as when it had to be temporarily stopped for benefit purposes. I accessed support from a local job broker and the Disability Employment Project who supported me in preparation for interviews, with Chris Morgan still supporting me from Community Mental health Services. I used this time to do something stress free whilst keeping myself busy, and the shop environment was perfect for this. In May of 2009 after a series of interviews for administrative posts I was successful with my application to work as an administrator. The job was full time, and I had several colleagues who could offer support as well as the office manager. I had to work at two bases both fairly close to one another. To start with I felt well supported, however a series of issues which caused severe anxiety triggered relapse, in the 22 months I did have to take some time off work. As I said previously suffering from a severe and enduring illness and coping with the demands of a full time job that normal Joe Bloggs would do, as well as any stressors out of work can be very challenging. On the first occasion the anxiety I felt (and tried to conceal) manifested itself in over checking things, which was picked up by my line manager who called me into a meeting with the manager who discussed this with me. Shortly afterwards I went home and they then realised that I wasn't well. I ended up seeing Dr Williams, a GP and getting a month's sick leave which was then to be extended for a further two months. The thing was with the health service that there was a lot of support from independent services, and although the anxiety I had was heightened significantly by the announcements of meetings with my line manager – at the time I thought – What does she want? Does she want to get rid of me? Is it going to cause me more anxiety? I was well supported. In that meeting I made sure that I had Chris with me, and the meeting went better than I thought it would have done had I not had him there with me. The focus was around my lithium level being low, something which the chief manager was able to see because of his experiences. The issue got resolved, my GP reviewed my medication and made adjustments and I saw Occupational Health who said that I should not have to undertake the most stressful part of my job, this being answering the telephone. They also said I should have a phased return, which was very helpful. The HR advisor and my line manager came to my home to explain this support. It was a very helpful and supportive way of getting me back into work even if in the long run I was to decide the job was not for me.

I spent a further few months there feeling fairly happy and well supported and following my trip to China to see my friend Matthieu where I flew to Shanghai and then into Yunnan Province (with him, his sister Amélie and a Chinese friend) and then from Shanghai to Beijing which I'm amazed to say I did alone not speaking a word of Chinese, I had an amazing time and was proud to say that I also overcame my anxiety of flying internally within China. The planes there are not that bad! The food did repeat on me but we stayed in some amazing guest houses and had adventures including having to cross ravines and stumble across places to stay in the middle of nowhere. In particular there was one guest house that I likened to paradise, where we fished our own fish for supper, ate passion fruit and had soft drinks on tap for £2 per night, and clean beds too!

On my return to the UK continued to work at the health service for a number of months and the work was so so, I struggled at times and did need time off on a few occasions. I realised however that some of the responsibilities of the work there did not match my skills set and were causing me anxiety so I made the decision in April 2011 to leave.

When I left the health service after a short period of ill health, I met with my line manager I handed in my notice. We did in fact have a good conversation after all and she told me that I had a really good sense of humour which made my day! I told her how much I'd appreciated the support she had given me including a work timetable I had in fact learned that I could express my views to help others and help them to know where they could improve things- there was no need to fear being honest. I'd also learnt more about what type of job I was best suited to.

Aside from any issues I had I felt at the end of this job, I took from it the experience I'd gained in administration, the credit card bill Id managed to pay off, and elsewhere the financial gains such as an occupational pension pot I'd started. I'd also earned enough money as stated above to visit Matthieu in China and then a further holiday in Tunisia the year after. I also knew that full time office work might not be the career path for me, certainly not with the health service. There were responsibilities as mentioned above that caused me serious anxiety including logging off members of staff and also getting hold of staff urgently or passing on urgent queries. I also learnt that I may not be totally suited to working in a confined space. But as stated above, it was by far from a disastrous experience.

Shortly after leaving the health service I did some temping night shift work for a recruitment agency and after a very helpful GP review who advised me to look at 9-5 work as the night shift work was affecting my anxiety levels, I sought help from Jen Bollands from the local Chamber of Commerce who provided excellent employment support and advice which led me to apply to work as an Assistant Gardener for Shaw Trust. I was over the moon when I was offered a temporary contract and following my holiday in Tunisia I started training for this. At this time, I'd talked to my CPN about a change of medication due to Olanzapine being very weight inducing, and he'd agreed to ask the psychiatrist who was a new consultant, to see me to consider this, after my holiday to Tunisia.

I had a great holiday in Tunisia, apart from the weather being very poor, I went quad biking and a tour of Carthage and Sidi Bou Said, a settlement of Andalusian descent.I also attempted crazily to have a look round one of the markets in Hammamet which was like being molested by a swarm of bees – I was the only customer there and the Tunisians were full on trying to get me to make purchases. I came back to the UK feeling more relaxed and ready to continue with everything.

Upon my return to the UK my relaxed bubble state was to be short lived, as I found out the health service organisation had over paid me by £1300 roughly. It was at this time too that I had started taking Aripiprazole, the anti psychotic that was to greatly reduce the weight gain I was suffering. I had been warned about it making me feel nauseous and dizzy which it certainly did. I took this drug for about a week, until in fact it made me feel physically sick, I remember when on the Assistant Gardener job (following leaving the health service) in the van and feeling so disorientated I couldn't look round to talk to them. I decided enough was enough and went to my GP who took me off the drug straight away – I hadn't slept well in a week. My GP was a very sympathetic and empathetic doctor who always listened to me. She had asked me if I'd heard back from the psychiatrist, I said no and that after my phone call on Wednesday I had rung Community Mental Health Services urgently asking them to get the psychiatrist to call me urgently- I stated that my GP was going to have to make significant changes to my medication. The response I got was from a secretary who just replied that the psychiatrist concerned was not available. I was really irate at this point and this was not this poor lady's fault. I agreed with the secretary that I would provide the GP with all information on my mental health, and I relayed all this to the GP who voiced the same concerns- she felt too that Psychiatric advice was necessary. I agreed with the GP I would go back onto 10mg Olanzapine and see the psychiatrist at my next follow up. The following day I'd had a phone call from an agency in London who had found my CV on one of the online job sites and had asked if I would be interested in being put forward for an interview at a local IT company. This recruitment officer was foreign- and from my opinion unbelievably critical. I sent her off various bits of paperwork – I was running around literally. It was true that at this point stress was getting the better of me. Anyway, this woman proved to be that bit too demanding for my patience, and I snapped – she had gone on about how I wasn't providing good enough answers and was continuously critical. The conversation cumulated in her saying "*Im sorry Andrew but I have serious reservations to continuing with you as your knowledge base is really not up to much.*"

"*Who the hell do you think you are*" I bellowed back. "*You've hardly given me enough time to prepare. How dare you insinuate I'm not capable? Do you realise what I've been through these last few days???!! I've been physically sick, I havn't been sleeping or feeling well, and YOU HAVE THE NERVE TO QUESTION MY ABILITY TO DO THIS JOB?*"
"Oh I'm sorry," she said. "*I'm really sorry. You should have told me that you've had health concerns and that you've been having treatment. And you must tell them at the, interview, they may make allowances for you.*"

I'd seen regularly a therapist since leaving a job in 2008. She'd got me out of a hole then but I had found that as time had gone on I didn't actually need her help. When I told her about my overpayment and how I'd felt leaving my previous office job, we had a disagreement about it- she was quite a strong person and put forward her opinion. I was however frantic in mood and my impulsiveness into complaining had taken off completely. She had however been a great help and very supportive to me and I have to take from our meetings the positives which included the long chats about how things were going and the massages.

It was then at this point that things kicked off with my neighbour's son. This young boy was by and large a very challenging and for want of a better of word cheeky yet quite vindictive boy. It was the night before my second job interview (I'd had a previous interview at this company) and was for the French speaking IT help desk position as detailed above, I had my bedroom window open and could hear him saying *"fucking this and fucking that"*, and playing loud music. Well I'd had enough, given the other stressors that I'd had off him on previous occasions calling me all names under the son and *"Gay boy"* and with the medication issue and overpayment stressors I went outside and shouted up to him to turn it down which was met with abusive language. The next day – the Tuesday I believe, I woke up and felt strange, I could smell a sickly sweet smell, of lemon. I remember going to the cash point- the truth is by this point I was feeling so ill with stress, and the sickness caused by the change of medication, that when I got home having been at the supermarket I started to have bouts of vomiting and called the doctor's who basically in a round about way were not too helpful. I went to work in a state and saw my line manager who was very supportive and told me to take off the afternoon, and I went again to the doctor's who were yet again rather unsure of what to do except to contact Community Mental Health Services. I ended up driving round to my parent's home and throwing up again. That afternoon a CPN contacted me at my parent's home after I had been sick again – the stress was about the complaint I'd made to the Police about my neighbour's son as well as the medication issues amongst other things. The CPN confirmed that things would have been easier had I not had such a volatile experience coming off Aripiprazole. That afternoon I went with mum to the Police Station where I filed a complaint about my neighbour, to the Police. The Neighbourhood Police had told me I would have to do this first of all – I found that the Police Officer to be helpful and understanding. He had however advised me to contact Environmental Health – which is stressful enough on its own! My neighbour's face was like thunder when she saw me following this. There was an awful lot going off and my health was in a really precarious state. That evening I felt really dehydrated and I had the sense to realise that I shouldn't take my medication as Lithium requires you to be really hydrated.

After speaking to the Out Of Hours Doctor she sent me to A+E and I sat in the waiting room where I was seen by an African doctor, my bloods were taken- surprise surprise my Lithium came back at 0.4, which is low- it should be 0.6-0.8. He told me in simple terms I should take my medication. I was by this point quite fed up and I started crying and said "*I do take it, I do I do, honestly.*" Of course the Lithium was low, it had been over 24 hours that I had taken it! He referred me to the on call duty psychiatrist who I had a chat with, he was a nice empathetic guy, said that given everything I had a lot on, then told me to take my tablets and sleep. I went home and awoke at 4.30pm the next day in the afternoon and spoke to my line manager who told me to take the rest of the week off. Following on from this, the next day I rang Sally urgently about the overpayment. I was told again that she wasn't available, so I pushed to get contact with her. At the time of Sally contacting me I was just about to go into to see the psychiatrist. I was in a very stressed state and my view of her was distorted as a result of this. Although this was not the case, in my mind I felt that she made me feel as though as I was a 'problem', an 'imposition'. "*So, Andrew, lots of contact,*" she said. I kept it together although I felt like lashing out- she said that she wanted to increase my Olanzapine as I appeared irritable – I said that I would rather not due to the fact that it is weight inducing, but she said that a small change would not make so much of a difference. She was alarmed when I said that I'd rather not but I ended up agreeing to it. The noise and harassment from next door continued and I overheard my neighbour talking about me to some other youths outside my house – I again contacted the Police as I was feeling very anxious about coming and leaving my home. The Police told me that she could not stop me opening my window on a hot sunny day. The video recorder I'd bought seemed defunct- it was so hard to film any of the abuse without being seen. That night was my friend Charlie's stag do, Id been invited and Tanya, Mary's sister had said I could stay at her's.

I'd also been trying to support her family as her mum was dying of cancer. So I went on the stag do and enjoyed myself, well tried to enjoy myself but amidst all the stress I recognise now it was probably no the best ailment. My car had been parked near to the family home and I had a dilemma, do I go back and face more issues from next door or drive to the caravan which was a fair distance being rather unwell? I decided I couldn't risk going back home given that Tanya was not available so I drove to the caravan site at Ashford in the Water. It was about midnight when I arrived upset and my parents asking me what was wrong. I was very agitated and left almost as soon as I got there. I drove down the road and suddenly became very distressed so I stopped in a small lay by near the entrance to the camp site. I put the hazard lights on and started sobbing. I decided that something had to be done so I rang and spoke to an out of hours nurse, but my battery was very low and I told her this uncontrollably. She said that she would stay on the line as long as she could but that I would have to call back if I got disconnected. To my good fortune a lovely Dutch couple staying on the campsite came over to my car and asked if I was ok. I remember this lady fondly, she was very calm and reassuring. Shortly afterwards a Police car spotted me and the Police men helped to calm me down. They asked me what had happened and I told them my situation, allowing the Dutch couple to continue their walk back to the camp site. While they were calming me down Tanya was ringing my phone, she had spoken to one of the Police men saying that she was very concerned about me. Initially I told them I didn't want to speak to her but then I realised it wasn't fair on the Police officers so I agreed to speak to her, as obviously she was concerned and when I spoke to her she wanted to sort things out with me. It was to my fortune that I had my medication on me, which I took then I had been speaking to the Out of Hours Nurse who then spoke to the Police and I sorted things out with Tanya and she very kindly let me spend the night at her home.

The next day I went to Out of Hours again over this weekend and saw a Dr Leyland who advised me not to go to the Police about the previous day's incidents as she said that it would aggravate the situation further, so I rang the Police and explained this.

The day after on the Monday I saw my CPN at Community Mental Health Services and told him what had happened and that I had also on this day been in to work and made a mistake which made me feel bad as I thought I had messed up and I felt as though I could not cope with things as they are. On Tuesday I saw my consultant psychiatrist who thought that I was experiencing a mixed affective state and she advised of a medication change – a reduction in Sertraline –in my eyes she appeared to be judging me about having had to drive on Saturday having been unwell and I felt looking back that this was something of serious concern to her. I went back to my CPN and told him this that she did not seem to have taken into account my situation at this time. I told the CPN that I was prepared to make a complaint against my psychiatrist about this. The CPN arranged for a meeting with my psychiatrist on the following Tuesday. When I arrived on this day at the reception after having a go at the receptionist for being kept waiting I told the CPN that I had decided I was going to put in a formal complaint against my psychiatrist- I couldn't see that the psychiatrist was only concerned with my health and safety. I went into the consultation room, I remember this meeting only too well – there were some bits I remembered better than others though. She was quite stern but I came back at her so hard in my response she retreated in her chair. The essence of it was that I'd decided my psychiatrist was also refusing to write a letter for me to show to the multi agency meeting that I was going to attend about my neighbours. But I hadn't understood why she was refusing – she wanted me to get more information off the Police so she knew exactly what she should say to

them. She was at this time in my clouded view making life more difficult by taking this stance- but I was not seeing things clearly and due to my irritability I felt she was acting against me, which was actually not what at all she would have ever wanted. I had various documents with me and I thrust the report that my GP had given me from the hospital that I had requested.
"Here, have a look at this. And if you've got a problem with that you can argue it out with my GP."
"You can have your whole notes, if you like." She coolly replied. (I did as a result of this comment go on to request my notes to the manager of the Mental Health Team there).
"Do you realise how many psychiatrists I have seen since diagnosis?" (I went on to list them), *"and you've not been seeing me regularly because you've been too busy swanning off on management leave!"*
In my irate state of mind I went on to say how offensive I found her. By the end of the heated consultation she was silent and looked aghast, the CPN had decided he agreed with her about my situation and I felt very alone. They wanted to reduce by Sertraline to 50mg and increase Olanzapine to 15mg. I asked for a change of psychiatrist, and then left – she had also said that she was going to stop me from driving by contacting the DVLA. Well my car was parked in the town centre so I wasn't going to leave it there! The consultant wanted my CPN to come and see me the next day, and that he would call me, however I was yet to play my trump card! When he called me whilst at Katy's I said in my angry state that I would not see him as I didn't think it was appropriate given he was supporting this doctor who I was complaining about. I had failed to see throughout all this that the psychiatrist was actually trying to help me get better sooner and she had been thinking only about my safety. Instead I just saw red due to all the stressors that were going on.

I went to my friend Katy's and told her what had gone on- that I wasn't happy about the care I was receiving and that I was making a complaint. We had a chat and agreed I would contact the duty GP who said given the circumstances I should stay on my medication and see my GP. On this day it was a Wednesday and the GP on shift - told me that the psychiatrist was doing what she was doing as she could be sued for medical negligence if she ignored the situation, but said I could stay on my usual tablets and ignore the psychiatrist's advice about not driving. Wow, great – I finally thought I was getting somewhere! I went away feeling quite satisfied – I had got the better of this psychiatrist! But had I - was I helping myself here?

But these brief moments of so called success were short lived – About an hour after I saw my GP the CPN rang, and said that the psychiatrist wanted me to see the Crisis Team. I said triumphantly that I had just seen my GP and that she disagreed with her, she had said that she felt I was well and said that I didn't need to agree to the medication changes that the psychiatrist was imposing on me nor did I have to stop driving. The GP had said too that for a mental health assessment to result in sectioning a patient all three clinicians – Consultant Psychiatrist and AMHP (Approved Mental Health Professional) have to be in agreement. The CPN and the psychiatrist then proceeded to contact the GP and presumably discuss their argument as to why I should have the medication changes and stop driving. The GP then contacted me to say that the psychiatrist had been in touch and that she was now advising me to have the Crisis Team assessment. If I refused to have the Crisis Team assessment then I could be subject to a mental health act assessment and ultimately be sectioned. As much as I was really cross and that I wanted to resist – I was after all putting a formal complaint in about her, I new that I was heading for trouble going down this route. If I were to be totally honest with myself I would know that she was in fact right about her justification for her decisions about my care. I ended up driving to Lincoln that day just to get away. On the way to Lincoln I stopped the car and found the number of a local solicitor who I rang, and when I arrived in Lincoln I spoke with a local solicitor who was made aware of the situation. She asked me if she thought she was trying to section me, and I said that yes I thought most certainly she was trying to do this. *"You've got to fully cooperate,"* she said. *"They can batter your front door down under various sections if required and drag you into a Police van if they have to."* I agreed with this advice that it was in my interests to cooperate even if as I felt very strongly I did not agree with or want any support from a psychiatrist that I was putting in a formal complaint about complaints manager said, this doctor could still make decisions about my care even though I was complaining about her. It seemed like an hour or so when my phone rang, this time it was an approved mental health professional (AMHP). At this time I was walking round Lincoln, I seemed to do this for several hours while speaking to various professionals.

"Hi Andrew, I was just ringing about these problems that you've been having with the psychiatrist, would you like to tell me about them," he asked. I told him about the incident with the car and the Police after having gone out for my friends stag do and how I had not wanted to return home due to the harassment and noise from my neighbour, and that I had entrusted this with the psychiatrist and she had been in my eyes quite judgemental and dismissive as she saw the problem being that I had driven having been not quite fit to drive, as opposed to the fact being that as my plans had fallen through I was left with no choice but to drive to my parent's caravan in the Peak District and if it hadn't been for the Police and Tanya I would have been in a bad way. I certainly did not want to go home given the problems with my neighbour. Again what I failed to understand was that the psychiatrist was only concerned about my health and safety and her motives had been misconstrued. I offered

to the AMHP an apology for the psychiatrist which I knew I needed to do. The AMHP said he would pass this on and that I see my usual GP, who was my usual GP with an interest in Mental Health. I told him spoken to a solicitor and my GP from university Dr Belfringham who had both been very supportive. Dr Belfringham knew me much better than any of the others, but like everyone she was only interested in my best interests – I knew I could count on Dr Belfringham for moral support which counted for so much at this time, to have someone endorse you at a critical time was worth its weight in gold.

I saw my GP with my friend Kathy Turnham present, Kathy is my next door but one neighbour and I class her and Daniel as friends. Kathy had always been there for me including previously when I needed to get a prescription for sleeping tablets late on, she had been good enough to take me to Out of Hours and then the pharmacy.

My GP assessed me at the local GP Practice. She asked if I could remember what happened when I was sectioned back in 2000, I said I could and explained it to her, and she then asked if I knew whether those thoughts were real to me now, I said absolutely not. She then proceeded to say that I'd held myself together throughout this nasty ordeal but asked me again if I'd agree to the medication changes that the psychiatrist was insisting upon and that I should see the crisis team. I offered to refer myself to the Hartington Unit, my GP however said that this would not be necessary. I realised that at this point I had no choice but to say yes, bearing in mind what had been said from the solicitors. The next day, I believe it was a Friday; I received a letter from the psychiatrist saying how sorry she was that I felt she had been dismissive of me! And she was sorry too I had seen so many psychiatrists, a point which I had said that she had not taken into account. I rang Dr Belfringham and told her about the letter and we had a good chat about things.

We had a long chat and talked about what was going on. That afternoon the Crisis Team came to assess me, Josie and Judy and they were lovely. Kathy Turnham, my good neighbour again agreed to sit in.

"*Have you been having suicidal thoughts?*" Josie asked.
"*No,*" I replied.
"*Have you had any psychosis, hallucinations or dillusional thoughts?*"
"*No,*" I replied again.

As the conversation went on, the Community Psychiatric Nurse and the Social Worker seemed doubtful that I was in need of Crisis Support.
I managed to keep calm throughout this assessment. Over the weekend I went to Craig's wedding reception, then I saw Judy on the Sunday. We had a chat about the psychiatrist issue and she said that it was not a mental health issue but an issue which affects people all over. "*You had had a skinful, and then the psychiatrist says something. We all do it, respond impulsively – I've done it, then wished I'd waited. We'll hopefully look to discharge you soon,*" she went on to say. I spoke again with Dr Belfringham as the Crisis Team had requested more information about this episode so I provided a statement for Mark, a CPN with the Crisis Team who Id got on so well with previously. Mark has since 2007 along with his colleagues at the Crisis Team been an amazing support and has always helped me in the ways that would be best for me. As already stated, Dr Belfringham had been so supportive to me too and had given sound advice.

That evening I felt things were turning sideways – the medication changes were kicking in and having an effect. My care had been transferred to another psychiatrist and Mark from the Crisis Team was at my next appointment. This is where I lost it, broke down. Id really had enough. Id along the way I'd asked for all my medical records at this point. The thing is when unwell some people with mental health issues do and say the things that when well like normal people they would not say – tell someone to their face something confrontational, rude or challenging – which is exactly the behaviour I showed the psychiatrist. Yes I had had a skinful but I decided I should write her a letter apologising too. I dropped the complaint against her but it was to be a while before I could get over challenging medical professionals. I confessed to all the complaints at my appointment and they put me on amber warning and I was able to reflect on the previous few weeks.

"When someone puts in a complaint, the worker has to distance themselves from it," he reassured me. At this point he held my wrist as a comfort. I had always seen eye to eye with Mark and he had always had time for me, his reactions and care were always appropriate and he was always so approachable and caring. The psychiatrist went on to say that when she had seen me she had noticed how frantic I was at a previous appointment, (when I had had the manager on the phone about my overpayment) which I felt was too much to take.

"Its not a reflection on you, Andrew," she reassured, *"more an indication of how your illness was taking over."*

I realised that all this complaining was actually quite destructive as it can easily spiral out of control.

The next few weeks I had regular appointments and Mark continued to see me from the Crisis Team, monitoring my health. After a shaky few days Mark came out to see me at home and noticed an improvement, I described to him at this point that I was 'homing in on things' and was less emotional. I gave Mark the information on my hospital admission and again I rang Dr Belfringham who said that my mood had changed due to the changes in medication. She said that I had been more unwell as a result of the psychiatrist's changes and that it was not a reflection on me. I often wonder what would have happened had I not reacted with such lability – could I have been ok on this level medication – 12.5 Olanzapine which the psychiatrist had said should be 15mg and also a reduction in Sertraline to 50 mg. This balance did not last and a few weeks later I made an emotional response to this change to my GP when I rang, very distressed –I told her how this balance was not working and I seemed upset and angry that I had been subjected to these feelings. However I did not realise that my mood was still not settled and this was why I was reacting in such a way. Evelyn was great with me, very supportive and helpful, and she listened to and understood what was going on – she had a great ability to fully empathise. When I first got to know her she would come to my home several times a week after the events of the summer of 2011 when my mood hadn't settled, then less frequently when things stabilised. Evelyn had taken over from my previous CPN given the unfortunate circumstances over the summer with all the incidents. We agreed too that I should always avoid getting in the car when feeling upset which is some thing to this day I agreed to. When my mood wasn't stable I spoke to Evelyn and saw another psychiatrist who helped me to realise how my actions were challenging and confrontational and proceeded to monitor things very closely and notify my GP of this. With what had happened with the previous psychiatrist I was still prone to outbursts, and wrongly it seemed to have made me more confident which from my doctor's point of view was actually a sign of illness. A sign of illness it was, but it also disenabled me to challenge open and honestly my situation as per the medication I was prescribed. Maybe that was the price I was paying given having been quite poorly? It was after all my decision to ask for a medication change originally. I had after all been through a lot, dealt with a hostile situation at home with my neighbour's son, a medication change which was not successful as well as stress from my old job due to a vast overpayment and confronted a Psychiatrist (who had questioned my mental health and was considering a mental health act assessment on me) with a formal complaint. I think above anything else it had made me realise that I had dealt with a lot and that life doesn't have to be half that complicated. I learnt that a change of medication for me was not in my best interests (although for some this may be different) and that I would have to find other more helpful ways of losing weight, which was the reason I had requested a medication change. I also learnt how sensitive I am to medication changes and how fine a balance the medication is and how easily that balance can be upset and now I realise that my quality of life could not be better than it is on the medication that I take currently. I also over time learnt that being labile with others is really not a good idea – many can react badly to this and it can wreck or severely damage many relationships. Moreover, I learnt that it is important to pick your battles and be aware of how stress builds up when you start picking arguments with people and how waiting before reacting straight away if you perceive anything said or done to be negative – so you can think outside the box.

I was very labile on one occasion with another GP when I rang him asking him for a second opinion on my medication and so apologised to him then had a few run ins with other medical professionals - I found it hard when going to appointments and read into the negatives I saw in this consultant resulting in me reacting negatively. This confrontational behaviour cumulated over the period where I had multiple stressors occurring. It became my belief that I could be overly confident and assertive (i.e. wreck less to get what I wanted!) by being cross with people. Confidence however isn't about being confrontational which is where I went wrong, and it certainly is not about aggression. Because once you have caused chaos by shouting and being argumentative, there are consequences. I realised I couldn't go round making others feel uncomfortable. The price I paid for this confrontation was to not be able to be open and honest when there were issues that needed discussing, and that these things are not always easy to decipher. I was trying to make the point that even though I had been confrontational I felt I'd been labelled as a problem patient who was not worthy of being open and honest. As previously stated, I had learnt that it is usually better to wait before responding impulsively and as said to pick your battles. But positively speaking I'd shown the courage and confidence in bringing these issues to the attention of those concerned through the channels I was entitled do so. It is however also important to note that you must as previously stated pick your battles – there is always the risk that the stress associated with complaining can extend onto other issues where the outcome is less favourable, whilst it could also be demonstrated that looking for a suitable solution which in my case was simply to request a change of psychiatrist. Negative emotions feed of each other, and complaining can of course be very destructive.

Following this I had made positive progress with voluntary work – I'd signed up to work with the British Red Cross at the Refugee Service, and I'd started a building course. I'm not sure to this day why I'd signed up for the Building course but it had been a choice I made given the way my job had gone at the health service. It was a real chore going down there to the Building College and I guess for most of the time I hung in there as the people on the course were not really my cup of tea! Some of the lads on the course were into drugs and I really felt a bit isolated. Plastering and Painting and Decorating were ok –I managed to skim a ceiling which to this day I am very proud of. Although I was not gifted at wall papering and I didn't warm to Joinery or Plumbing. The tiling part of the course was very short and by the end of the course there were only about 4 of us still on the course – some of the others had had to leave as the Job Centre had forced them into paid work. Im not quite sure why I chose to do this course but if nothing else it increased my skills set and served as an introduction into a completely different career. My interests however definitely veered towards the voluntary work I was doing at British Red Cross. The Refugee Service work was for me my bread and butter at this moment in time, I enjoyed going on a Wednesday and sometimes Thursday to help Refugees - the main things that could be offered were things like bus tickets to Home Office appointments in, food vouchers or bags of food. There were requests for money sometimes which we had to refuse but it was extremely rewarding work – on one occasion I helped refugees from across Europe, some of whom who had been reduced to suicidal thoughts, so that they could to get housing support via Social Services. Generally speaking there was lots of support from the Refugee coordinator and case worker at this time. I also assisted refugees who were fleeing civil war to get financial support to live in the UK. I was there for about 15 months, and was awarded a commendation for my efforts where I attended a ceremony. It had been when all said and done a very enjoyable experience.

One day in August of this year I was driving back from the Red Cross when I was hit in the rear by a local driver. It was a massive shunt and when I got out of the car I was shaking. My first words to the driver was that did he not think to brake, he was in fact apologetic and soon afterwards the Police arrived and confirmed he was liable for the accident. He admitted this and we exchanged details. I made the decision that as I suffered a jaw injury and fear of driving I would pursue legal action against the driver. So I had to go for various medical assessments, physical and psychological where the physicians agreed that injuries had been incurred. My solicitor notified the third party insurers and after a bitter dispute whereby she had to issue proceedings as the third party insurers decided to challenge the medical evidence, they then agreed to pay for psychological treatment and compensation. The process itself is quite lengthy and to anyone who has been in a car accident and wishes to pursue a personal injury claim, it is quite a lengthy process, but if life event stressors throw you off course and you can recover to lead a stable existence, it may be something that you may wish to consider. For me when I started the claim I had no idea what I was letting myself in for and so it caused a lot of anxiety. One of the particulars that the insurance company tried to argue was that given I suffer with Bipolar, I was already anxious and unwell before the accident. But however when I saw the psychologist he had read all my medical notes and had confirmed that I was usually in good health but that life events could impact badly on me. My solicitor reassured me that they were liable and bound by this and the report confirmed that I had suffered psychological damage as a result of the accident. It was a learning curve for me and I certainly learnt more about this process and that in fact, being completely legal, there was nothing to worry about.

In October 2012 having worked as an Assistant Gardener I applied to work as a volunteer at local charity and I started by contacting members of the public to complete specific assessments. I enjoyed this too and was line managed by a lovely bubbly girl called Hannah who was very kind and supportive. Just before I started at this charity I also found some brilliant voluntary work at a local country house in the gardens. It was great to work out doors, doing jobs such as weeding, planting of seeds, raking, clearing trees etc. I continued this work along side the British Red Cross. I left the British Red Cross in January 2013 and went on to volunteer for a local library, alongside doing the voluntary work for a local charity. This was a short placement and I started it shortly after starting my teaching course at a further educational college nearby – this was to teach English to Speakers of Other Languages. I made some good friends on this course and the tutors were friendly and helpful and were very experienced. I gained a lot from the training and passed all my lessons. I realised that I was passionate about teaching and helping others to learn. The students were keen and it was great to meet foreigners from all parts of the world. I learnt all about how to go about teaching the lesson- task before text, and how students need to hear and say words before they see and write it. I got on well with Mary and Cynthia and they were very supportive. The course lasted 5 months which I successfully passed, and was offered an interview for a teaching job there. However I'd also had an offer of an interview for a charity, a paid job doing helping carers of disabled and disadvantaged persons – and this was a permanent job. I was successful which made my day – I'd really enjoyed working with the team at where I was volunteering – Hannah, Khylie, Beatrice, Robert, Kienna, Betty and Dina – it is a really nice supportive organisation to work for. My line manager Jennifer made various adjustments to my hours and after a few alterations I became happy on 20 hours. Im currently advertising my private tuition online and I have signed up with a tutoring agency. While working at the charity one of my tutors there asked me if I'd be interested in doing some volunteer ESOL teaching. I arranged to work this round my hours at the charity and from September 2014 to December 2014 I went every Tuesday and Thursday lunchtimes to New College to teach a group of foreign students which my line manager at the charity very kindly let me do. It definitely kept me going and I gained valuable teaching experience at lesson planning, use of resources and answering difficult questions. At the end of the term my tutor took me out for coffee and gave me a card with £50 in it! I was so happy that I'd felt appreciated. I had got on really well with Mary throughout the course and job and she had been a great support, as had Cynthia. I'd had to miss a couple of days due to sickness and a meeting at work but I was very happy that I'd been able to help out and gain some invaluable experience. I'd been doing well so far at the charity. I'd been doing assessments – interviewing members of the public to ascertain what emotional and financial support could be given, as well as sign posting carers onto other services. I'd also been doing Emergency Plans – these are in case the carer has an emergency, a support package can be put together so that anyone who should is cared for is looked after in an Emergency. In September of 2014 I'd planned to go and teach English in Saudi Arabia, and had also met a lovely guy, Jamie who Id been totally upfront about the Saudi adventure. We'd met online and then he was meant to come to see me for the weekend. Id been up to see him the night before to meet him and have dinner, it was going so well... Until the next day when he messages me and said he couldn't get involved because of my plans to teach abroad. Why did I have to stuff it up with the Saudi job? At this time I'd had my medications adjusted as my new consultant had wanted to reduce my Olanzapine to 15mg, this happened as the Jamie saga was unravelling unsurprisingly as these things usually do. I took two weeks off work to get myself better. The thing that I have always found with taking time off work with Bipolar issues is that I always dreaded coming back to work for a return to work interview-don't ask me why – well actually I can probably tell you why. From a very early age I perceived threats when people would talk behind closed doors, that they were talking about me. While off sick as previously stated I perceived that "management" would all be talking and discussing my ill health and how bad it was I was off work and what would they do with me when I went back. So in fact work became a catalyst for fuelling anxiety. This has been something that my mum in particular has been able to understand very well.

The Saudi teaching opportunity turned out to be nothing more than a financial nightmare, at least initially anyway. The agency concerned ended up not fulfilling its promises – in fact there were two agencies involved, one of them fought really hard for all the candidates to get their deposits back. It would be a lie to say it hadn't caused a lot of stress, it had in fact really upset the balance. After I realised that going out there would not be profitable given the length of time the agency had taken to process my application I pursued the agency for a full refund. I did in fact have two heated discussions about it and after I was promised a full refund which never occurred I went to the small claims court. Initially the agency defended themselves but after I investigated online about the sale of goods act and unfair terms and conditions act 1999 I realised that the terms and conditions they were using to defend themselves were in fact totally unfair. I sent all paperwork to the court and the defendants and then waited. Sadly they did not pay up still so the court awarded in my favour following their lack of communication. I was then forced to contact the County Court Bailiffs who attempted to contact the agency. Luck was on my side however that the partner agency at this point emailed me to say they had been asked by many other dissatisfied candidates to chase the agency concerned for refunds. After several attempts by the bailiffs and badgering by the partner agency, I did get my deposit back £500 thankfully but I had paid bailiffs to recover the deposit, it was a mere £130 which I agreed to write off. It was getting to the point where I just had no more fight left in me and I met with mum one day in November and she said I had to now think of my health. It was that very much day that the partner agency emailed me to say they had managed to secure a full refund of my deposit, and could they have my bank details to send the payment to! What a nice twist of fate that was eh? Since this point, after having been disappointed with the first date and overcoming the effect of the medication changes, I got to know another guy. He was fun to get to know, handsome and it appeared that he was very easy going. We started dating just after I had got over a previous fling and when I had made a claim for the £500 refund. We embarked on a nice relationship, meals at his home, meals out, I met his mum and sister at Christmas 2014 and we all seemed to get on so well. However there were cracks appear and certain things would trigger it. Initially I thought it best just to let go of any difficult situations comments or awkwardness ness but at times it was quite challenging, I tried to see the best in him as much as possible. He was after all a very funny and fun loving guy. He was quite tactile and in spite of scaring the living daylights out of me in some ways and making me feel on edge –I wanted the relationship to continue. We did argue quite a lot however and this did really upset me a lot. After discussion with my CPN she restored some faith in myself that it was ok to feel like that. He told me at home that he no longer wanted to continue seeing me as he felt the relationship had become very intense. I was gutted. I guess I still held something for him at this point. We continued seeing each other as friends but from my point of view it wasn't working and I felt rightly or wrongly it was not a comfortable relationship at times. I told him I did not want to continue being 'friends' and so severed the contact with him. It was sad as we did at times make a good couple in some ways but we just weren't compatible in others. His tidiness and my untidiness did not co-exist well as we both walked on egg shells round each other. I didn't want that for eternity! Anyway let's just say that we had a difference of opinion on quite a few things! I knew that all these issues were getting in the way of the relationship and towards the end I think the arguments killed the attraction between us. I did feel a bit trapped at times and think this was mirrored by mooting thoughts of re applying to go and work in Saudi Arabia. The friendship ended and I was when all said and done relieved. I think the Saudi teaching opportunity was a mere 'escape' from my current situation with him and when the friendship finally came to an end I felt I had made the right decision. I'd realised he wasn't the right person for me. Looking for the right person when you're gay is not easy, especially in a relatively small town. Since I'd started dating I'd learnt a lot – it's important to respect yourself as much as the person you are dating. If they don't show equal respect for you, then this can have damaging effects and lead to an imbalance in the relationship. If someone happens to put unreasonable demands on you and expectations that are totally unrealistic and also more importantly unfair, you have to ask yourself whether this person is right for you, even if you are attracted to them. Each experience has taught me something. It has to. With my first relationship I made the unforgettable mistake of signing a joint account and letting him live with me near the end of the relationship. With this chap I perhaps allowed him to exert his insecurities onto me for fear of risking the relationship. But I guess it's about showing the courage to problem solve the issue to your benefit. Relationships are ok (and enhance your life) while the going is good. But if your partner presents traits that you find very uncomfortable, this can be very difficult to rectify. Staying in such a relationship and blaming yourself for other's problems does nothing for you. For sure you can work on your own weaknesses, of course which I have too but where the other party needs to be willing to do this too, otherwise this is where you have to ask yourself whether you'd be better off without them. You need to feel completely at ease with each other.

Shortly afterwards I ran into some problems at work, things got stressful and I felt trapped again. But it wasn't just me who was getting it, my colleagues were too. In the autumn of this year morale at work was at rock bottom. Things were not adding up with my figures and I was feeling the pressure. This however was the beginning of the end for me at this employment. I'd gone from doing a role that I really enjoyed to an administrative position which gave me unfortunately less job satisfaction. The job I'd been comfortable in I was no doing, I did not feel I could continue with the stress levels as they were. I ended up going off sick and handing my notice in. Work seemed to be surprised as to why I'd handed in my notice, but I just felt that I'd enough. Whilst I was ready to move on from this role I miss to this day all my colleagues and we still meet up from time to time. But one important lesson that I learnt was that jobs may have a shelf life – everyone may reach that point where they've had enough, things get too much or there is too much pressure. At the end of my employment for the local charity I was celebrating various things –this was the longest I had been employed in a job, and also I had savings to fall back on which came in very useful when waiting for financial help to kick into action. The impact on my mental health was significantly lessened in comparison with previous occasions and I was certainly more in control. Nevertheless I needed support which the Crisis Team provided- some reassurance which was all that was required and I was discharged in about a week's time. It was noticeable too that from meetings with them though that I was requiring less and less support. In 2005 I required help for suicidal thoughts, 2007 and 2008 for extensive work related stress. In 2009 and 2010 again I required support, and again in 2011. In 2012 I suffered a car accident, again requiring help, and then in 2014 with a work related issue. What I'm trying to say is that through perseverance, dedication and effort you can get there with a mental disability. You gradually get better at dealing with similar occurring experiences and so your confidence will naturally increase. It can be hard, particularly at the beginning of starting employment but I'm testament to the fact that any obstacle, no matter how big can be overcome. Whether you've succeeded or failed – you've actually still succeeded as you've either done well or learnt something new about yourself. The only obstacle that cannot be over come where we fear overcoming an obstacle. Fear is a natural emotion, everyone has experienced it at some point in their lives but unless you go ahead and challenge it you won't achieve anything and your confidence won't increase. Everyone needs support from time to time and people who suffer with Bipolar Affective Disorder or another severe mental illness may need that bit more, but you can get through it and accomplish anything you want to if you really want to regardless of the mental health condition you have – well look at what happened to me and I'm now as strong as ever!

Chapter 6

CONCLUSION

When I look back, the stress caused at this latest employment has actually enabled me to continue on my recovery journey. I was able to take some time off, re assess things – start some self employment initiatives and look at further jobs. I take pride from the fact that I have always been compliant with my medication and this has in fact backed me up when in times of need. I'm grateful for the financial support I have received and for the support of my friends and family in moving forward. I was financially worried about things, leaving a job because of the effects on my health is one thing but then having to justify months and months off sick is quite something else. I didn't feel on this occasion that my state of mind was such that I should be signed off work for months. Instead I took a gamble with the self employment; it wasn't if honest my ideal work but was something I could get my teeth into – life is after all about taking risks and then re-assessing situations.

Since leaving the charity work employment in September I have started self employment for a health promotion company, taught languages (French and Spanish) in Primary schools for a Specialist Teaching Agency across the Midlands and have completed my NVQ qualification to help students achieve vocational qualifications in college, namely Health and Social Care and Business Customer Service. I am also looking forward to the prospect of teaching French and Spanish in After School clubs. I'm glad to say that I feel much less like complaining! And I maintain excellent rapport with the medical professionals. My mood is more balanced, I feel much calmer and more positive. How have I got here? By taking each day as it comes, one step at a time – pushing myself (a little but not too much), challenging negative thoughts by with positive actions taking reasonable risks, being compliant with medication, seeking medical help when un well at an early stage, taking on board advice from all medical professionals, attending counselling sessions, self-reflecting, doing plenty of exercise, self soothing strategies – (massages and Indian head massages are great), relaxation and meditation too where possible and being careful with money - saving some where possible and investing wisely. Most importantly though I have progressed by learning lessons. I also have learnt that you must pick your battles, complaining is very stressful – it is very important to look at what outcome you hope to achieve. It is also essential that you help yourself – as my sister Jackie told me, advice can be given from various parties but the most important part comes from you. I have some amazing family and friends who have supported me over the last 16 years and beyond-these being my lovely Mum, Dad, sister Jackie and brother in law Channa, step brother Matthew and sister in law Amanda (and their respective families) and Uncle Bob who I would like to thank for all their support and interest in what I have achieved and friends Tom, Jen, Katy, Marisa, Paula and her mum Judy for all their help and encouragement – as well as David and his sisters Sammy and Leanne, mum and dad Veronica and David and Steve for their utter loyalty and solidarity as well as and my Spanish friends Cristina and Luis and French friend Matthieu and his family for their support and understanding and amazing holidays out to

France, Spain and China! All these friends and family members and others too have helped me along the way to realise what great opportunities there are out there and that sometimes you have to have some bad experiences to experience the good. You don't necessarily have to go through what I went through, only look at my example and take lessons from it. And be brave, proactive and strive to get better – no-one else is going to do it for you.

I've just completed 4 days training to be a sales negotiator for new home builds and have been offered a job selling educational courses to parents of children requiring learning support. If I'm having a bad day I put on Paul Mckenna's Instant Confidence cd a few times or I go down to the gym and before I know it I'm feeling better, and this to has enabled me to manage my condition better by managing the next few days better and avoiding a relapse. We all have times when we reach burn out point and need support and this is perfectly normal, so to get on track a bit of support helps us a long way. I'm no longer requiring regular support from a CPN and I see my psychiatrist less often. I've realised too, most importantly that in order to keep well, I need to stay on the same dosage of medication – 1 gram of Lithium, 20mg of Olanzapine and 150 mg of Sertraline as I've learned that I'm extremely sensitive to medication changes. Putting pressure on yourself can only impede your progress. I've not relapsed since I made this decision- my quality of life could not be better.

You can make anything happen if you want it to. Don't ever fear failure as it enables you to succeed; you see there are two shadows of success. So what's stopping you?!

ABOUT THE AUTHOR

As a sufferer of Bipolar Affective Disorder I have as everyone else has been on a journey which has had both major ups and downs. My hope is that this book will give hope and reassurance to those in crisis with mental health concerns and those looking to make the next step in progressing with their lives, and that it will provide some lessons by which the reader can learn and be aware of. There is no perfection in life – we can only strive to do better.

Lightning Source UK Ltd.
Milton Keynes UK
UKOW02f0022130716

278255UK00001B/51/P